$\overset{\prime}{\mathcal{M}}$

# A DISTANT PROSPECT

# A DISTANT PROSPECT

*Lord Berners*

A SEQUEL TO
*First Childhood*

TURTLE POINT PRESS
AND
HELEN MARX BOOKS

*A DISTANT PROSPECT*
*Turtle Point Press and Helen Marx Books*
*1998*
*Copyright © Lord Berners c/o The Berners Trust*

LIBRARY OF CONGRESS CATALOG NUMBER 98-60327
ISBN 1-885983-32-8

*Design and composition of text by*
*Wilsted & Taylor Publishing Services.*
*Design of cover by Lawrence Wolfson*

*Cover Image: Frontispiece to* Taylor's Perspective, *1760, detail,*
*William Hogarth*

CATALOGING-IN-PUBLICATION DATA

Berners, Gerald Hugh Tyrwhitt-Wilson, Baron, 1883–1950.
   A distant prospect / Lord Berners. — 1st pbk. ed.
        p.      cm.
   "A sequel to First childhood."
     1. Berners, Gerald Hugh Tyrwhitt-Wilson, Baron,
   1883–1950—Childhood and youth.    2. Novelists, English—
   20th century—Biography.    3. Diplomats—England—
   Biography.    4. Composers—England—Biography.    5. Eton
   College—History.    I. Title.
   PR6003.E7425Z465    1998                    823'.912[B]
                                               QBI98-1053

# CONTENTS

CONTENTS

*Ah, happy hills! Ah, pleasing shade!*
*Ah, fields beloved in vain!*
*Where once my careless childhood stray'd*

. . . . . . . . .

*I feel the gales that from ye blow*
*A momentary bliss bestow,*
*As waving fresh their gladsome wing,*
*My weary soul they seem to soothe,*
*And, redolent of joy and youth,*
*To breathe a second spring.*

Thomas Gray,
*Ode on a Distant Prospect of Eton College*

# A DISTANT PROSPECT

# I

## *Goodbye to Elmley*

❖

In the spring of 1897 I was fourteen and a half. The time had come for me to leave my preparatory school, where I had spent over four years, to go to Eton.

It was commonly believed at Elmley that when you went to say goodbye to the headmaster and take your leaving prize, invariably a volume of Scott's Poems bound in crimson morocco, it was his custom on that occasion to give you a little lecture on the mysteries of sex.

In my case the initiation was not forthcoming. Mr Gambril spoke to me very earnestly about my future, about my duty to my God and my Country, about the importance of games in the development of character, and he regretted that I had not done better in this respect. He warned me against allowing music to interfere with my studies. He quoted Longfellow, "Life is real, life is earnest." He spoke to me of this and of that, but there was never a word about sex. Whether he considered that I was not yet ripe for so portentous a disclosure, or whether he was not feeling physiologically inclined that morning, I shall never know.

I was a little disappointed at not getting something I had been led to expect. At the same time I felt relieved—just as when one goes to the dentist, braced up to bear the expected pain, and is told that the tooth will be dealt with at the next visit.

I must confess that I had been a little alarmed at the prospect of the revelation. I had a presentiment that it might be going to add a further responsibility to my already sufficiently complicated life. I had anticipated it almost with the dread with which, in the Legend of Glamis, the heir might be supposed to look forward to his initiation into the family secret.

As far as matters of sex were concerned, Elmley was an innocent school. No doubt the state of terror in which we were kept by Mr Gambril checked all tendency to prurience. In any case, boys who may have been sexually enlightened kept their enlightenment to themselves.

In those pre-Freudian days it had not yet been discovered that children experience the stirrings of sex at a very early age. Their innocence in this respect was taken for granted. Now we believe them to be little sponges of iniquity, absorbing matter for horrible repressions, and, as beliefs have a way of conjuring up realities, perhaps children of the Victorian age really were more innocent than those of the present day in whom even the "clouds of glory" are darkened by the murky fumes of sex. I am sure that in my own Recollections of Early Childhood there were no Intimations of Immorality. There had been many delightful things to engage my childish curiosity, but sex was not one of them. I soon discovered that there were certain subjects which seemed to cause embarrassment to grown-ups. There were incidents, too, such as dogs being suddenly shouted at and torn hastily apart, and I can remember being hurried away by my nurse from a cow that was about to have a calf. But these things inspired repulsion rather than curiosity. No doubt I was an unduly prim child. I certainly gathered the impression that this mysterious thing which seemed to inspire so much apprehension and disapproval in my elders was distasteful in its nature, and that I should not have gained any pleasure in knowing about it. I never deliberately embarrassed my pastors and masters with awkward questions. It had never been necessary to delude me with pretty fables of storks and gooseberry bushes. Nor did I ever come across anyone who, unsolicited, seemed anxious to give me any information on the subject.

As I left the headmaster's study, clasping my volume of Scott's Poems to my bosom, I could hardly realize that I had gone out of that den of torment for the last time, that the great day of deliverance had come. Time, at Elmley, had seemed to move so slowly that it had almost assumed the quality of eternity. I had looked forward passionately to this day, which never seemed to be getting any nearer. Now that it was actually at hand I could scarcely believe in its reality. I wondered how I could make the most of it, and thought it might not be a bad idea to celebrate my last day at school by trying to reverse in the sense of joy all the miseries of my first.

After packing my meagre effects and saying goodbye to the Matron there was still an hour left before my departure. Most of the other boys had gone away by an early train and the school was nearly empty. I decided to take a last look at all the spots connected with the most unpleasant memories of my school life. The idea was ingenious but not wholly successful. I opened the door of the class-room of one of the assistant masters I had particularly disliked, to thumb my nose at the interminable hours of boredom and bullying I had spent there, but in its emptiness it seemed to have completely lost its ominous character. I walked out into the playing fields, the scene of so many humiliations, but here again painful recollections were dissolved by the soft sunshine and the mild breezes of the early spring morning. I climbed up on to the roof to view the scene of the disastrous incident that had put an end to my friendship with my idolized hero, Longworth. But I only succeeded in evoking a sentimental resurrection of his memory. On my way down I was tempted to abandon this thorn-extracting process and take a last glimpse at the dormitory I had occupied one summer term when my friendship with Longworth had been at its zenith. That particular summer stood out in my memory as one of the few periods of my school life when I had been comparatively happy. During convalescence after a slight illness I used to sit up in my bed as evening came on, gazing through the window at the placid landscape fading into darkness, my heart filled with nostalgic yearning. I hoped to recapture the emotion. When I entered the room I found Creeling, a boy I very much disliked, peering out of the window. "Hullo," he said. "You know, I've always liked this view. It's pretty, isn't it? I was just taking a last look at it."

Many years later, when I was sketching in Rome, a

grim-looking Englishwoman came up to me and said with some asperity, "I see you are painting MY view." That the wretched Creeling should be admiring "my" view was intolerable. The discovery of a community of taste in landscape did nothing to reconcile me to Creeling. He was one of those smug kind of creatures whose agreement on any point immediately induces a change of opinion. I also realized that we should both be leaving by the same train, and that the pleasure I was anticipating from the journey would be spoilt by his presence. It seemed as though the ghosts of Elmley were conspiring to spoil my last moments there.

After this, I renounced any further emotional experiments and began to make my way slowly to the station, preferring to wait on the platform rather than risk any further encounters. I might even see Mr Gambril again.

Elmley station was about three hundred yards from the school, perched on an embankment that skirted the playing fields. From this platform one could survey the whole of the domain. Beyond the playing fields, through the straggling line of elm trees, were visible the grey stucco Georgian house, the chapel, the gymnasium and the fives courts, and in the distance a low line of wooded hills. The prospect, enveloped in a soft golden haze, had the appearance of a nineteenth-century aquatint of a "Gentleman's Seat."

I had not experienced much happiness at Elmley. I loathed the headmaster. I had made few friends. I ought to have felt an infinite relief at bidding farewell to the place for ever. Yet, as I gazed for the last time on a scene that, in the last years, had grown as familiar to me as my own home, I was overcome by a sense of melancholy which culminated almost in tears. I realized that, in spite of the many humiliations, disappointments and hardships I had suffered there, I had acquired a genuine affection for the place. Its personality, at the moment when I was about to leave it, seemed to have detached itself from its inhabitants and all the human memories associated with it, and to have become endowed with a friendly charm of its own.

In addition to this, I experienced for the first time in my life the sensation of growing older, and for the first time I was conscious of the poignancy of bidding farewell to a period which, unpleasant as it had often been, could never be re-lived.

## II

## *The Holiday Tutor*

❖

On my horizon there had appeared from time to time a little cloud which had as yet assumed no very definite shape—the question of my future career.

Mr Gambril had written to my mother recommending her to send me into the army. He considered that, for a boy of my temperament, a military training was essential. "He has many good qualities," Mr Gambril conceded, "but his character sadly needs bracing up. The army would make a man of him."

The suggestion filled me with alarm. As far as I could make out, the army seemed to be merely a continuation of school life, an existence of dreary routine presided over by colonels like the assistant masters at Elmley and generals like Mr Gambril. Happily, my mother did not favour the idea. She had a prejudice against the army, due to the fact that a member of her family had contracted pneumonia and died in the Crimean War. (My mother was addicted to associational superstitions. She would never go to Florence because a favourite aunt of hers had died there. She was sure that if she went to Florence she would die there too.) She was equally opposed to my going into the navy. Although I had often heard her express the opinion that sons should follow in their fathers' footsteps, in my case she seemed to think differently. My father was in the navy, and, as he and my mother didn't get on very well, she disliked the idea of my being more under his control than hers. I didn't understand her motive at the time, but I was none the less grateful for it. I had no wish to go into the navy.

The call of ambition, if I heard it at all, came to me not as a trumpet blast but as the horns of elfland faintly blowing. I looked forward with scant enthusiasm to the prospect of any profession other than an artistic one, and this I knew to be out of the question. I was given to understand that it would be necessary for me to earn my living. I was surrounded by people who seemed to have nothing to do but amuse themselves, and I thought it grossly unfair. Why couldn't my grandfather, who was immensely rich, provide me with sufficient money to enable me to live in luxurious ease like my uncles and my aunts? What was the point of becoming a grown-up gentleman if one had to be bothered with a profession?

My mother had a very elementary knowledge of the world that lay outside the domestic sphere. She knew that the army and navy were suitable professions for gentlemen. About other vocations she had only the haziest ideas. She thought highly of clergymen, but she had no wish for her son to become one. Neither did she very much fancy law or finance. She disliked the family lawyer, and the bank manager wrote her impertinent letters when she was overdrawn. She was hard put to it to think of an appropriate career for me. Eventually inspiration came in the shape of an elderly diplomat, a distant cousin, whom my mother had invited to Althrey. He brought with him an important-looking red despatch-box containing official documents—diplomatic secrets, no doubt. He had a pompously official air and he would occasionally insinuate that the welfare of Europe depended largely on his activities. When, later on, it came to relying on his influence, it turned out that he was of no very great importance. However, he managed to impress my mother and inspired her with pleasant day-dreams of her son as a future diplomat, with a red despatch-box and an official air. And so it was decided that I should go into diplomacy.

I knew very little about diplomacy. Enquiries convinced me that it was quite a nice sort of profession. It entailed going abroad, which I passionately longed to do, if only to get away from an environment that seemed to be exclusively composed of relations, schoolmasters and organized games.

For the moment I was confronted with the more immediate business of preparing myself for the Eton entrance examination. The Reverend Ernest Prout had been procured by Mr Gambril to coach me during the holidays. It was a great nuisance that the holidays should have to be spoilt by the presence of a tutor, but I was anxious to do well in the examination. I hated Mr Gambril and I suspected him of thinking poorly of me. I was all the more determined to prove to him that I could be a credit to the school. It seemed a way of getting even with him.

Throughout the holidays I worked feverishly—the thought of it now inspires me with a certain ironic amusement—to pass into an institution that was to render me incapable of working seriously for many years to come.

Mr Prout was an assistant master at a small preparatory school. The fact that he was a clergyman had led me to hope that he might perhaps resemble dear Mr Bevis, the only assistant master at Elmley for whom I had felt any affection, or Mr Allen, the curate, so like Jesus Christ in appearance, who had taught me Latin as a child. But Mr Prout proved to be a very different kind of person. I took a dislike to him from the first moment I saw him. Even the aspect of his luggage in the hall before I caught sight of its owner filled me with apprehension. It seemed to exude smugness. As for Mr Prout himself, his features were expressive of a medieval asceticism enlivened by a horrible ecclesiastical brightness. He looked like a bad Cranach daubed over with a shining varnish of Victorian complacency, a Gothic church restored in the late nineteenth century. His thick-set, rather corpulent body was surmounted by a head that ought to have belonged to a taller, thinner man, and his hair was parted in the middle and smoothed down with Macassar oil. His scraggy throat was animated by an Adam's apple which, when he spoke, bobbed up and down like a float. He appeared to suffer from indigestion and his speech was continually disturbed by ill-concealed flatulence.

I don't think that even my mother was very favourably impressed by Mr Prout. When I asked her if she liked him, she gave me an evasive answer. Except in a case of flagrant delinquency, she would have been as loath to say anything to prejudice me against clergymen as to criticize Queen Victoria or a Conservative Prime Minister.

My mother hardly ever discussed politics, or she might have discovered that Mr Prout was a "horrid radical." Once when he spoke of the "idle rich" she said, "Oh, but, Mr Prout, all the rich people I know are always very busy. They always have a lot to do."

"I don't count hunting or shooting," Mr Prout replied, "or going to parties."

"Why not?" my mother asked, and the subject was dropped.

Another time, after visiting some people in the neighbourhood whose house was surrounded by a very fine park, Mr Prout remarked, "I look forward to the day when such parks as these will be divided up and given to the poor." My mother exclaimed, "Oh, Mr Prout, but what on earth would they do with them?" I don't think she attributed Mr Prout's expression of opinion to his political views, but only to the implications of Christianity.

Mr Prout seemed anxious not to be taken for a clergyman. He dressed himself up in sporting tweeds and secular checks. But it was of no avail; he was irrevocably stamped with the ecclesiastical die. His voice and his manners were unmistakably clerical. He had a lively fund of clerical slang and was always saying that things were "awfully jolly." He professed to be very keen about games and reproached me for not being more interested in them. He said that the only point he had in common with the ancient Greeks was his predilection for athletics, and that games brought him into closer contact with young people. There was perhaps another point he had in common with the ancient Greeks, for I subsequently heard that he succeeded in getting himself into closer contact with young people than was thought desirable by the school authorities. I noticed that he was rather persistent in his demonstrations of affection. He was continually patting my head or stroking my hair. However, I suffered this embarrassing friendliness with a good grace. I only wondered if it might not perhaps have something to do with a ceremony I had read of in the Prayer-book called The Laying on of Hands.

Luckily Mr Prout's peculiarities did not interfere with his capacity for teaching, and I passed the Eton examination with considerable success. This, I may say, was my swan-song as far as examinations were concerned. Since then I never succeeded in passing any other.

Throughout the holidays I had concentrated on my work and tried as far as possible to put out of my head all thoughts of music. Mr Gambril had persuaded my mother that frivolous artistic pursuits would surely encompass my downfall. I had hoped that on leaving Elmley I had done for ever with Mr Gambril, but it seemed as if the evil that he did was going to live after him. No doubt according to Victorian standards of male education he was right. The aim was to promote manliness and gentility, and music was neither manly nor gentlemanly.

Although my mother discouraged my artistic leanings, there were at the same time indications that she had a sneaking sympathy with them. She liked to hear people praise my amateurish piano-playing and my still more amateurish drawings. She was willing to tolerate my gifts as long as they remained on an amateur level. But the thought of any son of hers becoming a professional artist filled her with horror. She herself had learnt to play the piano and paint in water-colours. She used to play to me when I was a child and allow me to look at her sketch-book, but as soon as I began to show signs of developing talents of my own, fearing perhaps that she might be calling into being a Frankenstein's monster, she put away the sketch-books and closed the piano.

My mother's culture, like her character, was full of contradictions and confusions. In her schoolroom she had acquired a taste which, with the cocksureness of her

Victorian mentality, she believed to be the last word in artistic refinement, and for many years she continued to quote the opinions of her governesses on aesthetic matters. Sentimental associations, too, were important elements of her taste. She was inclined to be influenced by the opinions of people of whom she was fond. She liked the poems of Longfellow and the landscapes of Leader because her mother had liked them. It was difficult also to shake her conviction that the things she knew about were superior to the things she didn't, and priority of experience seemed to have for her a special significance. If she preferred Lewis Morris and Sir Edwin Arnold to William Morris and Matthew Arnold, it was probably because she had read the former first and because the person who had recommended them had been dearer to her than the one who had recommended the latter.

My mother appeared to think that literature and painting were less dangerous to me than music. She encouraged me to read respectable standard works, and whenever we were in London she took me to the National Gallery and the Royal Academy. My favourite authors at that time were Dickens, Thackeray, Rudyard Kipling, Rider Haggard, Anthony Hope and Marie Corelli. A book that I had been crazy about during my last term at Elmley was George du Maurier's *Trilby*. Mr

Gambril had confiscated it, but my mother had seen no harm in it, although for a long time she had not allowed me to read *Vanity Fair* on account of Becky Sharp. Among the painters I most admired were Raphael, Greuze, Lord Leighton and Turner. There was a picture I had seen in the Royal Academy called "The Doctor," by Luke Fildes, which had moved me deeply. My taste in painting was inclined to be literary. I liked a picture that told a story, and it was on account of his mythological subjects that I liked Lord Leighton. My ideas about art were influenced by a periodical my mother took in called *The Magazine of Art*, which nowadays makes curious reading.

Of life in general I knew little beyond what I had learnt at school and in the home circle, two of my most interesting deductions having been that people were always trying to stop one doing what one wanted to do, and that it was wiser to find out what people thought about one's opinions before expressing them.

Such was the culture and philosophy with which I was equipped at the time of my going to Eton.

# III

## *Eton*

❖

The anxiety I usually felt when about to confront an assembly of unknown fellow-creatures was much alleviated by the accounts I had been given of Eton—not by the kind of old gentleman who says that his schooldays were his happiest, but by contemporaries of mine who were already there. When I arrived, accompanied by my mother, on a sunny May morning, I was further heartened by my first impressions of the place. The gay and friendly appearance of the High Street, its attractive-looking shops, the neat eighteenth-century houses, their window-boxes bright with spring flowers, the lofty chapel masked by trees, a glimpse of the wide expanse of the Thames as we crossed the bridge, the grey silhouette of the Castle dominating the town, and the pleasant Georgian façade of Mr Oxney's house covered with jasmine and wistaria, combined to give me the assurance that the place could harbour nothing very alarming.

When my mother and I were shown into Mr Oxney's study I was for the moment disturbed by its resemblance to that of the headmaster at Elmley. But Mr Oxney himself was not in the least like Mr Gambril, and I instinctively knew that his amiability was not, like Mr Gambril's, just put on for parents.

Mr Oxney had an earnest expression, a high forehead and a heavy moustache. His face looked as if it were divided into halves; the upper half was that of a scholar or a clergyman, the lower half that of a military man. I was a little disconcerted by his earnestness, and I was soon to discover that, coupled with a complete lack of imagination, it was apt to make one's relations with him a little difficult. A sense of humour was markedly absent. I don't suppose that in the course of his life he had ever seen a joke, and, just as people say they have never seen a ghost because they don't believe in them, Mr Oxney never saw a joke because he didn't believe in jokes.

In all other respects Mr Oxney's beliefs were almost too well grounded. His convictions about every aspect of life, particularly the knotty problems of good and evil, were based on foundations as solid as those of a monument, but one often had doubts whether they were always situated quite in the right place. Yet, with all his earnestness and his firm beliefs, Mr Oxney was the type of man who seems predestined to exercise no influence whatever on anyone. He could chide and punish as efficiently as any other housemaster and could be quite ferocious at times, yet in spite of the firmness of his convictions he was utterly unable to convince.

"You would no doubt like to see your son's room," Mr Oxney said to my mother. He conducted us through a green baize door and left us in the hands of the Matron, a refined and rather gushing lady.

The boys' part of the house was a labyrinth of dark passages and staircases, and looked as if it had been adapted from the original structure on the principles of a rabbit-warren. Boys of fourteen are happily unconcerned with hygiene, and I thought it looked very nice and homely, at the same time rather romantic. It reminded me of the servants' quarters at Arley, the scene of many a delightful exploration in my early childhood.

The room that had been allotted to me was minute and garret-like—"a room," my mother said to me afterwards, "that I would hesitate to put even a pantry-boy into." I was less unfavourably impressed. It seemed to me a snug little den. The foliage of a plane tree growing in the courtyard outside cast a pleasant green glow on the walls and the ceiling, giving the room the rustic air of a summerhouse or a potting-shed. For the moment, however, it looked rather bare. It contained nothing but a bed that shut up into a cupboard in the wall, an uncomfortable-looking armchair, a small chest of drawers surmounted by a bookcase, known as a "Burry," a traditional Etonian piece passed on like an heirloom from one owner of a room to the next. The Matron gave my mother the address of a furniture shop, and we went off to buy a few *objets d'art* to give my room a slightly more luxurious air. My mother chose for me a set of sporting prints which I accepted without protest as a concession to popular taste. My own taste was asserted in the purchase of some Japanese fans and a large coloured photograph of a Tea-house draped in wistaria. I was at that time going through a Japanese phase inspired by a comic opera, "The Geisha," which I had seen in London during the holidays, and my ideals of beauty centred in kimono-clad mousmees, chrysanthemums and Fuji-yama.

When the time came for my mother to return to London I was not at all loath to part from her. I watched her train leave Windsor station with very different emotions from those I had experienced four years before on the

platform at Elmley. Then I had felt like a fledgling abandoned by the mother bird. Now I was eager to return and
confront the new life that was before me. In the last four
years I had gained a little in self-confidence; that is to
say, I had acquired something of the technique of self-
preservation, the mixture of bluff and cunning that en-
ables the physically weak to steer their way through
dangers and difficulties. There still remained the one
weak spot in my defensive armour, my inefficiency in
the matter of games. However, I understood that, although at Eton, as at Elmley, games were considered to
be the supreme test of moral and social excellence, there
were possibilities at Eton of evading them. One could, I
knew, take up rowing instead of cricket, one could become a "wet-bob"—and rowing, as long as it was not too
strenuous, was one of the forms of outdoor exercise I
most enjoyed. It was pleasant to think that I should be
able to boat on the river and "cleave with pliant arm its
glassy wave" instead of spending long dreary hours on
the cricket field. As I walked back from the station I
paused for a while on the bridge, and, looking down on
the river sparkling in the sunlight and animated with in-
cipient river life, I offered up my *Prière sur l'Acropole* to
Father Thames.

# IV

## The Matron, the Household
## and Two Friends

❖

My youthful instincts of association often deluded me
into thinking that people were agreeable just because I
met them in agreeable circumstances, with the result
that friendships begun with enthusiasm were liable to
end in disappointment.

O'Sullivan and MacBean were the first boys in my
house with whom I became acquainted. Their rooms
were on the same landing as mine. They were both of
them slightly older than me, and they had come to Eton
the previous Half. O'Sullivan came into my room, presumably to inspect me, and, having decided that I would
do, went to fetch his friend MacBean. Nobody until then
had bothered about me, and I was flattered by this

friendly gesture. O'Sullivan was Irish and MacBean Scottish, as their names might imply. O'Sullivan was small, vivacious and rather dirty; MacBean larger, cleaner, but of a more sombre disposition. If O'Sullivan could be compared to a little ray of Irish sunshine, Mac-Bean resembled a Scotch mist. They were neither of them in appearance or character particularly prepossessing; however, the two boys were transfigured by the roseate brightness of my first impressions of Eton. When we walked down Keate's Lane into the open country beyond, the fine weather, the rural intimacy of the landscape, the novel sense of liberty threw me into a state of ecstasy which included O'Sullivan and MacBean.

During the outing it was suggested that we should mess together. I was a little puzzled by the proposal, and it had to be explained to me that it meant having tea together every day in one or other of our rooms. I assented heartily. I thought that there could be no more enticing prospect than that of having tea every day with O'Sullivan and MacBean. When I got home I wrote to my mother and told her that I had already made two delightful new friends.

In a very short time, however, the delightfulness of my two new friends began to wear a little thin. O'Sullivan, for all his brightness, was incredibly stupid and te-

dious. He was perpetually boasting of the remarkable
sporting feats he had achieved at home in Ireland, feats
that I felt were too remote to be verified and too uninteresting to arouse any wish to do so. He was narrow-
minded and inclined to be censorious. Had he been more
powerful, I suspected that he would have been a bully. I
was increasingly irritated by his pointed pink face and
mouse-coloured hair that grew in a vortex. His antipathy to washing himself was very noticeable, and his
room had a musty smell that I found a little nauseating. I
minded MacBean less, but he was gloomy and taciturn
and held rigid moral views. He went so far as to confess
to me that one of his aims in life was never to say or do
anything that might cause his mother or his sisters to
blush. When I saw them I thought that he could allow
himself a fairly wide latitude. They didn't look as if they
were given to blushing.

My antipathy to my two messmates was further increased by the discovery that neither of them was popular in the house. More and more did I come to regret
having linked my fortunes with theirs. There was little
doubt that the fact of my having done so was proving an
obstacle to my making other, more desirable friendships,
and I noticed that one or two boys I singled out as being
more worthy of my affection seemed a little cautious of

responding to my advances. Yet I hadn't the strength of mind to break with my partners, and the dreary trinity remained for the time being undissolved.

Outside my house, untrammelled by my connection with these two detrimentals, I experienced less difficulty in making social progress.

I was informed by some of the boys in my division that Oxney's was not considered to be one of the first-rate houses. When my name had been put down for Eton a few years before, it had the reputation of being one of the most brilliant, but since then it had apparently deteriorated. Certainly the boys at Oxney's, when I came to compare them with the boys of some of the other houses, appeared to me to be a rather drab lot, and Mr Oxney himself not very inspiring. Perhaps it was because his department was the Army Class and he was only interested in the boys in his house who were destined for military careers. In any case, he seemed curiously aloof. He presided at meals, read prayers, made occasional tours of inspection to see that the boys were behaving themselves. Otherwise he was not much in evidence. The Matron, or Dame as she was called, played a more important role in our lives.

The discovery that Oxney's was not a first-rate house didn't worry me overmuch. It might be an advantage, I thought, to be in a house where the standard was not too high. There was less likelihood of my being continually harassed by the idea that I was not "playing up," that I was "letting down my side." Elmley had cured me of any desire I had to cut an heroic figure in school life. Now my aspirations were to remain as far as possible unobserved and not to be called upon to exert myself unduly in doing things for which I had neither the inclination nor the aptitude.

During my first days at Eton I had to concentrate on learning the various regulations of the school. They were mostly of a negative order. You were not supposed to walk on one side of the High Street, to turn down the collar of your change coat, to furl up your umbrella, to button the bottom button of your waistcoat, to eat in the street, to sit on the wall outside the entrance to the school yard. Many of the rules seemed unreasonable, and their origins, like the origins of some of the Christian doctrines, dated from so far back that they had long been forgotten. But if you didn't wish to involve yourself in trouble or expose yourself to ridicule they had to be rigidly observed.

The Dame, referred to familiarly as "The Hag," was a middle-aged lady whose slightly anaemic appearance

was redeemed by a wealth of fiery-red hair coiffed mod-
ishly in the fashion of the day. She had a sensitive nature
and literary tastes, and she wore pince-nez. Her surname
was Elton, her Christian name Flora, and although she
was always addressed as Mrs Elton, she was a spinster. I
took to her at once. She was so very gushing and agreeable. She encouraged the boys in whom she detected literary and artistic tastes to come and chat with her in
her little sitting-room, which was crammed to bursting
point with artistic knick-knacks and books of poetry. She
had a passion for Omar Khayyam. Innumerable volumes
of FitzGerald's translation of the *Rubáiyát*, bound in vel-
lum, in velvet, in soft leather tied up with ribbons, lay
about on every table. She knew the work by heart and
would frequently quote it in her conversation. It was its
poetic side, I imagine, that appealed to her rather than its
philosophy, for Mrs Elton was deeply religious and believed in regeneration through suffering. "It is along the
path of suffering," she used to say, "that we walk to
God," a doctrine that seemed strangely at variance with
the hedonistic outlook of her favourite poet.

Mrs Elton had a schoolgirlish avidity for confidences.
She used to implore the boys to consult her in cases of
difficulty and trouble. Fond as I was of her, I felt that she
was the last person to whom I should have wished to un-

burden myself. Her sympathy would have been over-whelming, and the value of her advice nil.

As I have said, Mrs Elton had a deeply sensitive nature. Upon discovering one day that she was nicknamed "The Hag," she burst into tears. It happened during luncheon and caused quite a sensation. Although she was assured that the seemingly unflattering sobriquet had no hostile implications, that it was merely a generic term for every Dame in every house, this was no consolation to her. She thought that she at least should have been exempt. The discovery left a wound in her heart and she would thereafter sometimes refer to herself, with a bitter smile, as "The Hag."

Mrs Elton did not seem to be over-fond of her own sex. She often spoke slightingly of other Dames and made herself noticeably more agreeable to fathers than to mothers. However, she had one very intimate female friend, a Mrs Watkins, the Dame of an adjacent house. It was perhaps a literary friendship, for Mrs Watkins was also very fond of poetry and was believed to write poetry herself. Mrs Elton and Mrs Watkins were as inseparable as their respective duties permitted. They would take tea together and go for rambles in the country, presumably discussing poetry and "the boys." Mrs Watkins was not quite so refined as Mrs Elton. She had rather a peculiar accent and was overheard saying one day, as she and Mrs Elton were setting out on a shopping expedition, "I don't mind what it is so long as it's fairly chipe and in good taiste," a phrase which perhaps would have made a suitable motto for Mrs Watkins.

With the exception of one rather seedy male servant, the household at Oxney's was run by a regiment of women known as "boys' maids," middle-aged or elderly females who seemed to have been selected for their lack of physical attractions. "Incidents" had been known to occur in other houses, but at Oxney's I am sure nothing of the sort could have happened. The only boys' maid who was in the least agreeable to the eye was the one who looked after my landing, but any charms she may have possessed were neutralized by a chronic arthritis that precluded any kind of wantonness. The sound of her shuffling footsteps as she approached my door in the morning to call me is among the most distinct of my auditory memories of that period.

Sounds are for me just as evocative as tastes, scents or any other Proustian time associations. The rarefied vibrations in frosty weather, when it seems as if a damper had been lifted from the diapason of nature and distant cries, the barking of dogs, the clattering of carts take on a metallic staccato quality, bring back to me my childish delight in a clear frosty morning. The whistle of a far-off train at night, the wind moaning in the chimney, rain beating on the window-panes, sounds that I used to hear as a child lying in bed, still continue when heard in similar conditions to evoke a pleasant sense of romance and adventure enjoyed in comfort and security. On the happily rare occasions when I hear shuffling footsteps in a passage, my mind flies back to those first days at Eton and I am haunted by the ghost of a fear lest I might be late for early school.

# V

## *The Microcosm of Eton*

❖

At Eton the daily routine was far less continuous, less monotonous than it had been at Elmley. There we had to work for never less than three hours at a stretch without a break except to move from one class-room to another, while at Eton there were intervals between each school varying from half an hour to three-quarters; and whereas at Elmley there was only one half-holiday in the week, at Eton there were three. On Tuesdays, Thursdays and Saturdays the afternoons were free except for "absence," a word that in the illogical Eton terminology meant its exact opposite. One had to be present at a roll-call read out by one of the masters in the school yard. In the Summer Half, absence was at six o'clock to prevent boys straying too far afield—as far as Ascot, Epsom or London perhaps—in the course of the afternoon.

◆

At Elmley we were roused by a bell at six o'clock every morning both summer and winter. At Eton a boys' maid came and tapped on the door—just as at home—in summer at six-thirty, in winter at seven o'clock. Early school was about half an hour later. Coffee and biscuits were provided in the houses, but at Oxney's the coffee was so nasty that most of the boys preferred to rush out to Little Brown's,* a sock-shop near by, where one could get good coffee and the most delicious hot buns stuffed with a wad of butter. The thought of those buns was almost a compensation for early rising, and their exquisite flavour lingers on my palate to this day. If it seems to me that I have never tasted anything quite like them since, it is perhaps because, as the Germans say, "Hunger is the best sauce," for no raven was ever so ravenous as I, in the early mornings at Eton.

The coffee and buns were dispensed by a snappy young woman called Phoebe, in a tiny panelled room packed to overflowing with hungry youth. Her name and the place, I used to think, were suggestive of an eighteenth-century coffee-house, but the conversations that took place there were perhaps a little lacking in eighteenth-century elegance.

*Little Brown's, now the School Stores.

At a quarter past nine there was compulsory religion in the Chapel, of which my enjoyment was rather spoilt during my first Half by my having to sit opposite the picture of Sir Galahad by Watts. A recent acquisition, it was much admired, and was once referred to in a sermon as having a message of its own. The only message it brought to me was one of irritation. Sir Galahad looked like the worst kind of priggish House-captain, and if he had been at Eton I didn't think he would have been very popular. Even when I was told that Ellen Terry had posed for the picture it failed to reconcile me to it.

Chapel lasted for about half an hour, and after this spiritual fortification there was school till half-past ten, and again from eleven to twelve. The two hours' interval that followed was known as "after twelve," and it was generally spent in Pupil-room. Pupil-room, facetiously termed Puppy-hole, was a class devoted to the study of the Classics, and the master who presided over it was known as one's Classical Tutor.

At Eton the method of teaching the Classics was very much the same as it had been at Elmley. That is to say, no effort was spared to make them as uninteresting and as unprofitable as possible. It is to be presumed that the school authorities, in making the Classics the principal item of their curriculum, had some edifying purpose in view, but if they thought that the study of pagan modes of thought was going to be useful to young Christians, it looked as if the masters thought otherwise and were bent on diverting the attention of their pupils to questions of syntax. In their hands Homer became tedious, Horace commonplace and Greek Tragedy a grammatical Inferno; and they contrived that the longer works were studied in so piecemeal a fashion that it was quite impossible to understand what they were about. It may have been that I was unfortunate in the masters I was "up to," for, with the sole exception of Arthur Benson, they left me with the impression that they cared for the Classics as little as they cared for their pupils and were making use of the former to penalize the latter, an impression that was strengthened by the fact that the worst punishment they could devise was the copying out of hundreds of lines from Virgil or some other classical author. It is hardly surprising that most boys left Eton with an incurable dislike for the Classics.

To return to the day's programme: luncheon (or dinner as it was called) was at two o'clock. At Mr. Oxney's house the food was not very good, but whether this was due to Mr Oxney's aloofness, or to Mrs Elton's ethereal insouciance, or to the spirit of economy, I cannot say.

In the afternoon there was school lasting from a quarter to three till half-past, and again from five till six. "Lock-up," the curfew hour, when we were shut up in our houses for the night, varied with the seasons. In the winter it followed immediately after the last school. In the summer it was at nine.

Thus, in comparison with the Elmley routine, we had in the course of the week a good deal of leisure at our disposal. How did I spend mine? Not, I fear, in a way that would have been approved of by the pious author of *A Day of my Life at Eton.* I passed a good deal of my time sauntering in the streets or in the playing fields, bathing or going on the river, frequenting the sock-shops when I had money to spend. Later, when I had acquired a little more self-confidence, I used to go out sketching. This had to be done surreptitiously, as in those days it was a form of "slacking" that aroused contempt and hostility. However, there were one or two boys with whom I could go out on the river, moor the boat in a backwater and give myself up to art, without fear of being betrayed. I also received a certain amount of encouragement from Mrs Elton, and I used to submit to her judgment the little views I painted of Windsor Castle, Brocas Clump and other picturesque landmarks. Her criticisms were always very much to the point. "A little more blue," she would advise. "I always think a picture is nicer if there's just a touch of blue somewhere. And also I feel there might perhaps be a little more boldness."

It was all very well for Mrs Elton to recommend boldness. Boldness unaccompanied by technique is worse than useless, and technique is difficult to acquire without instruction. There were drawing classes at Eton, but I was not allowed to attend them any more than I was allowed to have music lessons.

Perhaps not much harm was done by my artistic urge being restrained. I don't suppose I should have gained very much from instruction in the arts, such as it was, in those days, at Eton. What was more serious was the effect Eton had on my capacity for work. It is admittedly difficult to inspire young people with a spontaneous desire to improve their minds. Their earliest impressions that work is a kind of penance imposed upon them by grown-ups are not easily dispelled, and are aggravated by the system of rewards and punishment. Too much stress is apt to be laid on work itself, and not enough on the incentives for working. There were a good many tears in my early reading, but as soon as I realized that there were nice books to read, I began to take pains. If it had been impressed on me that the study of Latin and Greek grammar was going to enable me to read Latin and Greek authors in the original, and that some of them were really worth reading, I might have been more willing to put up with it. I had, like most young people, a strong capacity for resistance to knowledge that I didn't think was going to interest me. At Elmley terror had kept my nose to the grindstone. In the more relaxed atmosphere of Eton, this resistance, coupled with a natural indolence, was actually encouraged by public opinion. Boys who worked hard were not admired. "Saps" were despised, and sometimes even persecuted, and most of the masters seemed to think more highly of success in games than in work.

The Eton of my day still retained its character as a school for the sons of the aristocracy, the ruling classes, country gentlemen and the higher military. It was appropriate that an educational system intended for the leisured classes should have something leisurely about it. It is to be remembered also that in the latter part of the nineteenth century a change had taken place in the educational purposes of Eton. More importance had come to be attached to organized games than to scholarship, and more attention given to the fostering of character than to the development of the intellect.

As if in accordance with the spirit of the times, many of those entrusted with the inculcation of this principle were more remarkable for their characters than for their intellect, and in one or two cases character verged on eccentricity.

The first master I was "up to" was Mr "Hoppy" Daman, a grotesque little man, whose antics, resembling those of a monkey-on-a-stick, combined with a most peculiar voice, made it impossible for anyone to take him seriously. A stranger visiting his division-room might well have imagined that knock-about humour was one of the subjects taught at Eton.

Then there was "Pecker" Rouse (so called, I imagine, on account of his odd hen-like gestures), who moved about with shuffling footsteps and a suspicious air, peeping, as Percy Lubbock describes him, furtively at the day, as though he had too often caught it in the act of insulting him. He taught mathematics, as far as I can remember. In spite of his diffidence, he was rather bad-tempered. I was told that he was totally incapable of keeping order among the boys in his house, and the sounds of tumult that could be heard therein as one passed by seemed to prove it. Mr Rouse was continually being subjected to booby traps and practical jokes. Strings were stretched across the passages in his house precipitating him into baths, and his umbrella was frequently filled with confetti so that he was enveloped in a miniature snowstorm when he opened it in the street. It was hardly to be wondered at that he was suspicious and bad-tempered.

Another comic figure was "Toddy" Vaughan. He was rather of the same type as "Hoppy" Daman, but his appearance was less grotesque and his manner more authoritative. I remember him chiefly for his ejaculatory voice and his clipped words. He would suddenly shout "Snuff!" at boys who were misbehaving (presumably a contraction of "That's enough"). In spite of his eccentricities there was not much ragging in his division. Once when he was hearing us recite Greek particles, the whole division roared out "Τοδέ," and this was the only instance of an attempt at ragging him that I can remember.

What exactly are the defects of personality in their masters that inspire boys to rag them? Certainly some kinds of physical infirmity, such as deafness and short-sightedness. Ferocity is not necessarily a deterrent, except to the very young. Some quite ferocious masters were ragged, while milder ones went unscathed—perhaps because ferocity arouses a sense of adventure, there being more excitement in ragging when there is an element of danger: A display of bad temper can be fatal to authority. I sometimes used to wonder if, at a public school, Mr Gambril might not have been ragged—a consoling speculation.

Of my division masters the one I liked best—again with the exception of Arthur Benson—was Mr Impey. Mr Impey had a genial manner, a prepossessing appearance and a reputation for wit. It must be as difficult for a schoolmaster as for a comic writer in a daily newspaper to keep up a flow of original humour, and Mr Impey's jokes had a tendency to recur. One of them, indeed, was so persistent in its recurrence that it ended by losing a little of its savour. The hot-water pipes in the division-room used to emit strange gurgling sounds. Whenever this happened Mr Impey would say, "Deep calleth unto deep at the noise of thy water-pipes." On referring to the Psalms I found that the word was not "water-pipes" but "waterspouts," but perhaps Mr Impey had access to a different translation. Notwithstanding the uneven level of his humour, everyone was grateful to Mr Impey for his efforts to enliven school hours—it seemed to prove an amiable disposition—and he was deservedly popular.

Mr Impey had a rather endearing idiosyncrasy. When boys made excuses he liked them to be ingenious. An ordinary excuse he would dismiss with impatience. Arriving late one morning, I complained that my watch was fast. "Then," said Mr Impey, "you are later than you thought you were." "No, sir," I replied. "My watch was not as fast as I thought it was." I believe that it was largely owing to this repartee that Mr Impey gave me a good report at the end of the Half, for I had not otherwise distinguished myself.

Dr Porter, the science master, was jovial and rubicund. Science as it was taught by Dr Porter was, to say the least of it, exciting. Nearly every experiment ended with an explosion, and sitting in the front row of his division was like being in the front line of a battle. My experiences in his division were perhaps responsible for discouraging me in the further pursuit of science. Being of a timorous and gun-shy disposition, I thought that it would be wiser to leave it to others more courageous.

Among my other division masters were Mr Bealby and Mr Belford. They were both ministers of the Church of England and they were known as "Jumping Jesus" and "Creeping Christ." Mr Bealby was lean, wiry and ascetic. He would come bouncing into the division-room, looking like an athletic curate about to organize a Gymkhana for the choir-boys. He was the only master I really disliked, and the dislike was reciprocated. On every possible occasion he singled me out for his acid clerical sarcasm, and once he was instrumental in getting my leave stopped.

Mr Belford, "Creeping Christ," was his antithesis in clerical style. He was portly, unctuous, and slow in his movements. He breathed deeply when he spoke, so that his utterances seemed to be inspired with divine afflatus. In his sermons he had a manner of pronouncing the words "Deadly sin" that made one almost hear the Recording Angel rustling his wings. If Mr Belford suspected any of the boys in his house of immorality he would enter their rooms at night, kneel down by their bedsides and offer up a prayer.

It was my misfortune that I never came into contact with any of the more notable Eton figures, such as Luxmoore, Ainger or the Cornishes, and that I only enjoyed for a brief period the tuition of Arthur Benson. The Half during which Arthur Benson was my division master stands out in my memory as the most profitable of my Eton career. He was a revelation of what an intelligent and sympathetic master can do for one. Sometimes at a music hall, after a series of mediocre turns there appears on the stage a performer, not in the character of his act very different from the others, of whom one exclaims, "Here at last is the real thing." On the educational stage

Arthur Benson was the real thing. Like Mr Bevis at Elmley, only on a higher level altogether, he had the power of infusing a life into the Classics that stirred the imagination even of the most recalcitrant. It was true that the subjects taken that Half were in themselves stirring: the *Bacchae* of Euripides and the Ninth Book of the *Odyssey*. But how different was his treatment of them from that of the ordinary classical master! We were not plagued overmuch with difficulties of syntax, our time was not wasted in the discussion of grammatical curiosities. Our attention was directed to the literary side. Under Arthur Benson, for the first time since I had come to Eton, I worked hard and enjoyed working. But alas! the interest he had aroused in the Classics was short-lived. The flame he had kindled soon died down when the fanning ceased, and in the following Half, with a return of the usual pedestrian methods, my enthusiasm relapsed once more into indifference.

It is with no little diffidence that I approach the majestic person of the Headmaster, Dr Edmund Warre. For all who did not attain to the higher ranks of the school he was a remote and inaccessible figurehead of scholastic dignity, a deity in college robes. Like the God of the Israelites he was sublime and terrible, making an occasional appearance as from a cloud, and withdrawing himself again into his heaven without anyone being the better for it. His heaven was all that heaven should be, furnished with Victorian virtues, paved with the salt of the earth. If he had a defect—although it can hardly be considered to be a defect in a schoolmaster—it was that he was perhaps a little lacking in imagination. He trod with lofty step the path of honour and dignity. But one had the impression that the path was a little on the narrow side and that any touch of fantasy, any deviation from an expression of orthodox opinion, would be brushed aside in the sweep of his robes and trampled on by his great boots.

For most boys the nearest view of the Headmaster they could hope for was on the occasion of the periodical visits of inspection he was in the habit of paying to the division-rooms, and these were as awe-inspiring as any of the apparitions of Jehovah recorded in the Old Testament. He would come sweeping in, his robes swishing ominously, his handsome ruddy features set in magisterial solemnity. Some wretched boy would be set on to construe and would almost always, under the tension of the ordeal, break down. The Headmaster would give a scornful grunt and sweep out again, leaving the whole division and the presiding master smarting under a sense of inferiority.

Arthur Benson had an ingenious device for dealing with these incursions. Doctor Warre, like his greater counterpart, was not without his foibles. He prided himself on having a more extensive knowledge of Triremes* than any other living scholar. Each time that he appeared in the division-room, Arthur Benson would contrive to bring up the subject of Triremes. Doctor Warre's countenance would immediately light up with pleasure. He almost bridled—if one may use such an expression in connection with so exalted a personage.

"Well, boys," he would say, "I suppose you all know what a Trireme looks like." He would then proceed to draw a Trireme on the blackboard and, becoming engrossed in his task, would invariably prolong his visit beyond the allotted time and be obliged to hurry away to inspect some other division-room. Construing had been avoided. The thundercloud had rolled away, leaving us unscathed. The Headmaster never failed to rise to the bait, and on Arthur Benson's face as he regained his desk there was a sly smile of satisfaction.

There was another presence, still more exalted, even more inaccessible than the Headmaster, yet more human and closer to our hearts, a greater Genius of the Place,

*The classical war-ship.

dominating it as Windsor Castle dominated the surrounding landscape—the little black bundle of majesty that we so often used to see trundling through the streets of Eton in an open barouche preceded by outriders. It was a sight that never failed to rouse a reverential thrill. We looked upon Queen Victoria as the real protectress of Eton, overshadowing "Our Henry's holy shade," and her statue outside the Castle gates, bad as it was, might well have been transported to the school yard to replace the effigy of our founder, by most of us passed by unheeded. We believed, rightly or not, that she had a particular affection for Eton boys, and in my daydreams I often fancied that had I, like the boy Jones, possessed sufficient courage and ingenuity to succeed in penetrating to the inner sanctity of the Castle, an Etonian trespasser would perhaps have been pardoned, and even welcomed with a few gracious words.

# VI

## A Musical Adventure

———

## Incursions into the Demi-Monde

❖

My relations with my messmates, O'Sullivan and Mac-Bean, became daily more strained. They had grown to dislike me as much as I disliked them, and while I attributed my failure to make any notable progress in popularity with the boys in my house to my association with these two, I also suspected O'Sullivan of indulging in hostile propaganda at my expense. However, no actual flare-up occurred, and as it seemed to be an unwritten law that boys who had arranged to mess together should continue to do so, the unholy alliance would probably have dragged on in an atmosphere of veiled hostility during the rest of the Half if it had not come to an end as

◆

a result of a curious misunderstanding of which I was the innocent and bewildered victim.

In the dining-room at Oxney's there was an aged piano, and Mrs Elton, to whom I had confessed my love for music, had given me leave to play on it whenever I chose. At first I hesitated to avail myself of this privilege owing to the promise my mother had extracted from me that I would not allow artistic pursuits to interfere with my studies. But the thought of the piano sitting there waiting for me got the better of my good resolutions, and one evening I stole down to the dining-room with a volume of Chopin's Nocturnes under my arm. Although the piano had acquired through age a harpsichord-like quality more suitable to Scarlatti than Chopin, the mere touch of the keys after so long an abstinence was a joy to me. I had not been playing long when the door was opened and a boy called Ainslie appeared. He was a most important person, a member of the Library, that Council of Ten that stood in the same relations to individual houses as "Pop"* did to the school in general. I jumped up from the music-stool in a panic.

He had not come to rebuke me, as I had feared. "Don't stop," he said quite amiably. "Go on playing."

*The Eton Society known as "Pop": a self-elected oligarchy of about two dozen boys having no official powers but immense pres-

He sat down on a chair near the piano and I played the Nocturne to its conclusion.

"By jove," he said, "I wish I could play the piano like that. Can you play anything out of 'The Geisha'?"

Fortunately I could. My taste in music had its lighter side and I knew a good deal of "The Geisha" by heart.

"That's the kind of music I like," Ainslie remarked. "Chopin's a bit morbid, isn't he?"

The shock of being appealed to in this familiar way induced me to agree with him. It was not the first time that I had heard Chopin stigmatized as morbid. The music master at Elmley had so defined him.

Ainslie went on to speak with enthusiasm of "The Geisha," which he had seen fifteen times. He also spoke with equal enthusiasm of Marie Tempest and Letty Lind, the leading actresses in the musical comedy.

It would be difficult for anyone who has not experienced the sacred solemnity of public-school hierarchy to appreciate my state of mind on thus finding myself, the lowest of Lower boys, speaking on equal terms with a member of the Library. I wished that O'Sullivan and MacBean could have been there to witness it.

---

tige. Members of "Pop" can wear stick-up collars, coloured waistcoats, roll up their umbrellas, walk arm-in-arm in the streets, cane boys in any house, a privilege denied to the masters.

It must have occurred to Ainslie himself that he had perhaps gone a little too far in unbending, for he soon resumed the lofty manner that restored the barrier of rank between us. As he left the room he addressed me in the tone of a royal command, "You will come and play to me again tomorrow evening at the same time."

On the following evening I went to the dining-room and started to practise all the light music I possessed, "The Geisha," "The Shop Girl" and some of the popular waltzes of the day. How fortunate it was, I told myself— hitherto I had been a little ashamed of it—that my musical taste had a more frivolous side that could be exploited to entertain the great.

When Ainslie appeared he was not alone. He brought with him four or five members of the Library, and among them Faulkner, my fagmaster. My relations with him were of a menial character. I emptied his bath, made his toast, took his trousers to the tailor's to be pressed. Beyond having once burnt the toast, I had given him no serious cause for displeasure. Yet his presence, together with all these grand people, filled my heart with fear. I felt like the boot-boy summoned to perform before the gentry, and my fingers trembled as I began to play. However, the music was easy enough and I managed to acquit myself with a certain brio. I also ventured to play some of the more tuneful Chopin waltzes, which were well received. Altogether the concert was a success, and I was commanded to play again on the following evening. It must be remembered that in those days gramophones were rare—certainly nobody at Oxney's possessed one —so that enjoyment of music was dependent on amateur talent.

It had been impressed on me by Mr Gambril and others that music was not the sort of thing that ought to appeal to nice manly Englishmen—but here was a conspicuous refutation of this theory. If music could appeal to such people as Faulkner and Ainslie, there couldn't be anything so shameful about it.

That I should be in a position to entertain the important members of my house was flattering to my self-esteem, but I felt it would be unwise to expect anything further. If my talent, like that of "Orpheus with his lute," had brought about a temporary unfreezing of the mountain-tops, it would be a mistake in any way to presume on this agreeable state of thaw. However, even if it led to no more favour than an occasional nod of recognition, it would be enough.

I refrained from telling O'Sullivan and MacBean or any of the Lower boys about these concerts, thinking that they might be irritated—indeed, I had not disclosed to anyone except Mrs Elton that I was able to play the piano. My discretion proved a grave error of judgment and led to unforeseen and damaging consequences.

It soon became apparent that there was "something up" between the members of the Library and myself. A friendly nod from Ainslie as we went in to supper was noticed and commented on. Other incidents of a similar nature occurred which seemed to indicate that I enjoyed a greater measure of intimacy with the Upper members of the house than was my due. As I had not explained the true reason for it, it was open to an interpretation of which, in my innocence, I hadn't the faintest suspicion, and I was at a loss to understand why I was beginning to be greeted with cynical grins and mysterious hints. I had the uneasy sensation of having got myself into an invidious position through no fault of my own. What exactly the position was I was unable to fathom, and I hesitated to seek for an explanation. It came, however, soon enough. O'Sullivan stopped me as I was going into my room and announced that he and MacBean had decided that they would no longer mess with me. In ordinary circumstances I should have welcomed this decision, but now it only served to increase the mysterious sense of guilt that was being thrust upon me.

"Why?" I stammered out.

"Why?" O'Sullivan repeated. "You know perfectly well why. Don't try that innocent stuff on me."

He turned his back and walked off down the passage, leaving me crushed under an insinuation of which I had at last realized the import. It seemed the bitterest irony that I should be suspected of a misdemeanour of which I was not only innocent but which was one that filled me with horror. In such a calamity innocence was no consolation. For the moment I could see no way out of the quandary. I could hardly request Ainslie and his friends to adopt a colder attitude towards me in public, nor could I ask Mr Oxney to announce a vindication of my character. Still less did I feel inclined to appeal for assistance or advice to Mrs Elton. I could only hope that eventually the truth would prevail and that it would come to be realized that the favouritism I enjoyed rested on purely aesthetic grounds.

This is what in fact happened. The existence of the evening concerts in the dining-room was verified, and the vigilance exercised by O'Sullivan and others having failed to detect any irregularities of conduct, my reputation was restored. However, the proof of my innocence didn't seem to bring with it any increase in my popularity. I suppose it was because people, when they think they have found out something to one's discredit, hate having to change their minds. Once the dog has been given a bad name—I seemed to have lost even that small measure of homage that virtue pays to vice, and I almost felt as if I had been guilty of trying to impose a fraud. The only thing I gained from this passing slur on my character was that I stopped messing with O'Sullivan and MacBean.

The episode had, however, a curious effect on my hitherto defensive attitude in the matter of sex. Now that the dangers of ignorance had been brought home to me in so personal a way, I felt rather foolish in not knowing more about it, and my former prudishness gave way to curiosity. I became increasingly disposed to make enquiries of those of my friends who were willing to give me the benefits of their experience. One of the most forthcoming among them was a boy in my division called Soames, a rather ugly pug-faced youth a few months older than myself but in worldly wisdom very much more advanced. He told me one day that he had actually made the acquaintance of one or two Windsor tarts and asked me if I would care to meet them. The suggestion appealed to me. At the same time I was a little alarmed, for although my interest in this newly discovered field of exploration was growing daily I was as yet far from any desire to realize it in a practical sense. Guessing perhaps the reason of my hesitation, Soames reassured me. "Of course," he said, "there'll be no question of doing anything with them. It would be far too risky. But it's fun talking to them."

We set out for Windsor one afternoon, and, at the corner of a street near the White Hart, I was introduced to Miss Ada Pearson, a flamboyant-looking blonde lady wearing a black lace dress and an enormous picture-hat with feathers in it. She seemed an amiable young woman and she talked to us quite as if we had been grown-up people. Her conversation, though slightly marred by a cockney accent, was extremely ladylike. We spoke of the weather. Miss Pearson said how very pleasant it was to go on the river in summertime, and she commented on the quietness of Windsor as compared with London. No, she had never been to Paris, but a gentleman had once promised to take her there. She had just observed the Queen driving by and thought Her Majesty was looking very well. Apart from the reference to the gentleman taking her to Paris, it was a conversation that might have taken place on any rectory lawn, and, except for the picture-hat and a rather heavily rouged countenance, Miss Ada Pearson didn't look very different from the other young women one saw walking about the streets of Windsor. Yet I was as much thrilled by her as if she had been one of the most famous stars of the Parisian demi-monde.

A few days later, Soames introduced me to another of his acquaintances, Miss Annie Wise. She was the daughter of one of the watermen and was much younger than Miss Pearson. She can hardly have been more than fifteen or sixteen. She wore short skirts, and her hair hung in a loose pigtail tied up with a large black velvet bow. She also wore a picture-hat, but it was smaller and less flamboyant than Miss Pearson's. Neither was her conversation as mature. It consisted chiefly of giggles and entreaties to "go on." She was a fragile-looking little thing with a china-like complexion, and she had an over-large, loose mouth that resembled a wilting sea-anemone.

"She's not actually a tart," Soames explained to me afterwards, a little apologetically, "but she's supposed to be all right."

Of the two encounters, the latter was less sensational but more romantic. Miss Pearson was more impressive, but in Miss Wise there was a mixture of innocence and wantonness that I found strangely moving. I was presented to Miss Wise in the dusk just before Lock-up, in the shadow of a clump of trees illuminated by the light of a street lamp, and for many years afterwards I continued to associate lamplit foliage, wherever I saw it, whether in

Hyde Park, in the Champs Elysées or in the Viennese Prater, with the mysterious pleasures of vice.

These excursions into the world of sexual immorality, though of a purely academic nature, brought with them, none the less, an exhilarating sense of superiority. I could now afford to smile at the naughtiness of the bad characters in *Eric* or *Tom Brown,* and I was pleased to think that I could always meet any charge of pusillanimity with the retort, "Well, anyhow, I know a couple of tarts."

However, these landmarks in the history of my sophistication were destined to remain only as lurid memories. In the way that such things happen in school life, Soames and I became estranged and my link with the demi-monde of Windsor was broken. When I saw Miss Pearson again she failed to recognize me, and I hadn't the courage to go up and accost her. Miss Wise vanished completely. It was probable that her father, the waterman, a man of austere appearance, had found out about her being "all right" and had sent her away somewhere out of reach of the temptations of the town.

I often used to wonder to what extent the more dashing of the Eton bloods availed themselves of the services of the Ada Pearsons and the Annie Wises, but I left the school before reaching a position of seniority that would have enabled me to make any serious investigation of the problem. Evidences of the form of vice more usually associated with public schools were not lacking, and I feel that I should not be doing my duty with regard to the truthfulness of my chronicle were I to pass over the subject in silence.

It is a subject that has been handled by the most highly esteemed authors of all times, from Moses to Proust, and sometimes, I may say, not without a certain degree of hypocrisy. You may recollect the words of Gibbon in the eighth volume of the *Decline and Fall*: "I touch with reluctance and despatch with impatience a more odious vice of which modesty rejects the name and nature the idea." After which the historian goes on to say: "A curious dissertation might be formed on the introduction of paederasty after the time of Homer, its progress among the Greeks of Asia and Europe, the vehemence of their passions and the thin device of virtue and friendship which amused the philosophers of Athens." From which it would appear that Gibbon did not find the subject as unpalatable as he would have liked his readers to think he did.

There can be no denying that in the Eton of my time a good deal of this sort of thing went on, but to speak of it as homosexuality would be unduly ponderous. It was merely the ebullition of puberty. It is of course advisable that these juvenile aberrations should be discouraged, just as are the other excesses of drinking, smoking and gambling. But they are not much more dangerous, and parents who have been distressed by reports of public-school immorality may be reassured. Boys who are genuinely homosexual will go on being homosexual whether they have been to a public school or not, and their pathological peculiarities will have to be dealt with by psycho-analysts or, if they are unlucky, by the police, while those who are sexually normal will soon abandon this kind of nonsense for the real thing. I can only say that, in all the cases of which I have been able to check up on the subsequent history, no irretrievable harm seems to have been done. Some of the most depraved of the boys I knew at Eton have grown up into respectable fathers of families, and one of them who, in my day, was a byword for scandal has since become a highly revered dignitary of the Church of England.

# VII

## *Marston*

❖

I had hoped that, having been relieved of O'Sullivan and MacBean, I should be able to embark on a new phase of social advancement in my house, but instead of this I noticed with growing concern that my unpopularity was increasing. The downward trend, which no effort of agreeableness seemed able to prevent, continued during my second Half, and by the end of it there were very few boys at Oxney's who would speak to me.

At first I attributed this state of affairs to the machinations of O'Sullivan, who, since the termination of our alliance, had become openly hostile. But he was hardly popular enough, I thought, to have succeeded in organizing so widespread a measure of ill-feeling, and I was reluctantly forced to conclude that my unpopularity was due to defects inherent in my character. My lack of keen-

⚬━◆━⚬

ness in the matter of games had no doubt a good deal to do with it. But that was obviously not the only reason. There were several boys just as bad at games as I was who were not unpopular. I was loath to believe that I was any nastier than many of the other boys in my house, I was not unduly conceited, bad-tempered or slovenly. I was always conciliatory in the expression of my opinions— sometimes, through consciousness of my physical weakness, a little too conciliatory. I think that perhaps—although I was not fully aware of it at the time—what most contributed to my unpopularity was that I was wanting in team spirit, that I was not what the Americans call "a good mixer," and among schoolboys a desire to "keep oneself to oneself" even for a few moments in the day is looked upon as a disagreeable eccentricity. Whatever may have been the cause of the dislike I had inspired in my house, it did not seem to affect those outside it. In my division, among the boys in other houses, I had many friends. Although it was consoling to find that I was not universally spurned, there were inconveniences attending external friendships. Lower boys were not supposed to visit boys in other houses, and intimacy had to be limited to the division-rooms and the open air, a limitation that was particularly irksome in the wintertime, when Lock-up was early, and the long hours of enforced solitude, spent in my room within earshot of the noisy companionship from which I was debarred, brought with them an intolerable sense of inferiority and loneliness. I longed to try and get myself transferred to some other house where perhaps I would be more appreciated. If only I were at Arthur Benson's! That was "the sweet golden clime" to which I aspired. The boys there seemed to be a far better lot than the dreary denizens of Oxney's, and Arthur Benson himself how far more inspiring than Mr Oxney. But when one is young it is not an easy matter to escape from one's environment. The process of changing houses would have entailed a good deal of awkwardness, such as offending Mrs Elton and having to confess to my mother that I was unpopular. Altogether too many difficulties were involved, and I knew that I should have neither the courage nor the energy to face them. And so the project remained merely a pleasant dream to beguile my moments of depression.

There was a boy in my division called Marston, a very odd-looking boy, whose appearance at first sight had not inspired me with any great desire to make friends with him. My ideals with regard to physique and clothes were those of many of the female novelists of the day, and in Marston there was little that conformed to normal aesthetic standards. He was of an untidiness that exceeded the limits of what is possible in a civilized community. His clothes looked as if they had been designed for somebody else, whom they equally would not have fitted, and his hair was so unkempt that one felt only a garden rake could have coped with it. His face was long and narrow, with a prominent aquiline nose, and his forehead was curiously lined for a boy of his age (he was about fifteen and a half). His eyes, flashing with intelligent vivacity, were so attractive a feature that they almost redeemed him from ugliness. His general appearance, had it been accompanied by diffidence, might have seemed repulsively squalid. But it was carried off with so fine a swagger, so complete an air of self-assurance, that a picturesque effectiveness was achieved which made me think of the pictures I had seen of Gringoire and François Villon.

It was not long before I realized that Marston had a dominating personality, and I noticed that he was treated by the boys in the division with a certain deference. I heard that he was renowned for his fearlessness in ragging the masters, and of this an example occurred within the first few days of the Half. The division master, Mr Belford ("Creeping Christ"), announced that he proposed, each morning, to open early school with a prayer, and that, while this was going on, nobody was to talk. He proceeded to recite the Lord's Prayer in an unctuous voice, but before he had got very far with it Marston put up his hand and asked, "Please, sir, did you say we *were* to talk or that we *weren't* to talk?" There was a hoot of laughter from the division. Poor Mr Belford looked pained and never ventured to repeat the experiment.

In a flash, the repugnance I had previously felt for Marston changed to the wildest admiration, and I decided I must at all costs obtain his friendship.

In the Autobiography of Alice Toklas, Gertrude Stein says that whenever Miss Toklas meets a genius a bell rings within her. Hitherto I hadn't noticed any bells ringing within me, but when I got to know Marston something of the sort certainly did seem to happen. Never before had I come across a boy so intelligent, so witty, so erudite, in his understanding so extraordinarily mature. At the same time he was very much given to childish fun and nonsense. He treated every situation with a humorous impertinence that enabled him to get away with many things that would not have been permitted to others. In his dealings with his superiors he was in the habit of indulging in a form of seemingly innocent repartee that reduced them to impotent exasperation, and the more prudent among them found it better not to "monkey with the buzz-saw." It was this side of his character that had at first appealed to me most, but I soon found worthier motives for admiration. It was through Marston that I made the discovery that intellect was not the solemn, ponderous thing I had believed it to be. Hitherto I had only heard the word "intellect" used as a term of reproach, directed against anything that rose above commonplace comprehension. I had come to connect it with such things as mathematics and the drier side of classical education. Marston displayed it to me bereft of all forbidding solemnity and showed me how it could flash and sparkle and agreeably illuminate.

I had often felt a hankering after more imaginative forms of humour than those I had met with at school and in the home circle, where such manifestations of it as occurred seldom rose even to the level of *Punch*. The only exceptions I had known had been my father and Mrs Harvey. But my father's wit was too cynical to be comfortable, and Mrs Harvey's too much alloyed with feminine frivolity and current fashion. With Marston I felt that I had at last come upon the real thing. He appeared to me as a creature of transcendent brilliance, coming from a sphere that was different from the rather com-

monplace and conventional one that was my own. That
he came from a sphere that was slightly different in a social sense I was also aware. He rarely spoke of his home
life. I knew that he was, in his own words, "in the fortunate position of being an orphan," and that he was in
charge of a guardian, whose detachment, he said, allowed him complete liberty of action. I also knew that he
lived in the suburbs of Wolverhampton, which didn't
seem to me to be an ideal place to live in, and that his father had been connected with commerce. One of the boys
in the division who didn't like him told me that his father
had been a grocer—which, of course, from the point of
view of an Eton boy of that period, would have been a
very terrible thing. However, I attributed this piece of information to prejudice and dismissed it. Nevertheless,
there were one or two little things about Marston, almost imperceptible nuances of manners and outlook,
that seemed to suggest that he might not perhaps be connected with a county family or with the aristocracy. Although the influences of my environment had given me
a slightly critical sense of social distinctions, my admiration of him was strong enough to overcome it, and I
was not offended by his occasional lapses, because they
did not seem to be indicative of genuine vulgarity but

merely the result of his not having moved among people whose manners and customs had the veneer of elegant hypocrisy. I was even less disturbed by his ignorance of the sporting vocabulary, by his speaking of a fox's tail, by his referring to foxhounds as dogs, though I trembled to think of what would have been my mother's reactions.

Marston had also some of the defects of precocity. His skill in argument, and the pride he took in it, often led him to take an opposite view for the purpose of exercising his forensic skill, and he was inclined at times to mystify, and deliberately to talk above one's head. As at that time there was a good deal of the "omne ignotum pro magnifico" in my standards of appreciation, I admired him all the more for not quite understanding what he said.

Marston introduced me to a great many books I should not, in the normal course of my development, have read at the time, and it was owing to him that I began to frequent the school Library, an institution that most of the Etonians of my day used to regard very much as the devotees of Bacchus might have regarded a temperance hotel. The place became for me a sort of haven of refuge, a sanctum into which I could be sure no members of Oxney's would be likely to penetrate, and I came to look upon its tawny book-lined walls as ramparts that protected me from the dangers and dullness of the Philistine world.

For the first time I had occasion to appreciate the distinctive atmosphere of a library. At Althrey there was no library, only a few bookcases that contained literature ranging from Dickens and Thackeray to Marie Corelli. The library at Arley was not so much a library as a living-room devoted to the activities of daily life. It was not a room to sit and read in. The books that lined its walls formed merely a decorative background, serving no more literary purpose than wall-paper or panelling and, although it had a peaceful air, the peace was too often disturbed by frivolous conversation or by the snores of my grandfather. As for the school library at Elmley, if it had any atmosphere at all it was that of a bookstall at a railway station, with a never-ending stream of small boys coming to take out or replace volumes of Henty, Marryat, *Chums* or the *Boys' Own Paper*.

In the school Library at Eton I had a curious sense of exhilaration and I seemed to feel myself more intelligent there than elsewhere. It was as though books by their mere presence in such numbers had the power of radiating the warmth of culture. When I spoke to Marston of this impression, he said that it was sufficient to have instructive books in one's room for them, even unread, to emit beneficent exhalations—to say nothing of the impressive effect they made on people who thought you had read them.

Marston had collected round him a small group of kindred spirits, four or five boys who, while not too seriously intellectual, were interested in things of the mind, a sort of schoolboy version of the Souls. We used to meet nearly every day in the school Library, where, clustered round a table in a secluded corner, we could chatter unheeded. The bond that united us was perhaps a similarity in sense of humour rather than a community of tastes. Marston was interested in literature, but cared nothing for music, while two of the group, Delmer and Wilson, who were fond of music, were fond of it in different ways. Wilson was a very good pianist and, like many executant artists, was more interested in the technique of execution than in music itself. He didn't seem to care what he played as long as it provided technical difficulties and enabled him to show off his brilliance. Delmer was chiefly concerned with the theoretical side of music. His taste was, to my mind, a little too intellectual. He was contemptuous of Chopin, to whom I was still as devoted as ever. "The man could never have written a good fugue," he said to me one day in the course of a discussion. Happily, in other matters than music Delmer was not quite so academically minded. On the subject of life he could be frivolous enough, and he had a lively sense of humour. But even in his lighter moments there was a touch of the governess about him, the more noticeable for being emphasized by his appearance. With his high forehead, his abnormally thick spectacles and the rather prim arrangement of his hair, he had the air of a German Fräulein.

There was nothing governessy about Wilson. He was of the impertinent type, and his bright little face had the alert expression of an intelligent fox-terrier. He was addicted to playing practical jokes, for which he had an ingeniously inventive talent. He had gained a certain reputation from having once penetrated into Lower Chapel and, after extracting the explosive tapes from a box of crackers, having fastened them inside a number of hymn-books in such a way that they would go off when the books were opened, so that the announcement of the hymn-number was followed by a salvo of explosions.

There was one member of the group, a boy called Johnson, who was not so bright as the others. In fact, he was not bright at all. The only features that redeemed him from being an insufferable bore were that he was quite nice-looking in rather a bovine way, that he was extremely good-natured and that he was appreciative of other people's jokes when he could understand them. He had conceived a wild admiration for Marston and no amount of snubbing and cold-shouldering could discourage him. He had an insatiable thirst for knowledge and never stopped asking questions. Marston said that he wielded notes of interrogation like a bludgeon. He was a bit of a drag at times on the vivacity of the conversation; however, he was convenient as a butt, and in this capacity he earned our toleration. When one couldn't think of anything interesting to say, one could always turn on the unfortunate Johnson.

My friendship with Marston and the frequentation of his group contributed a good deal towards brightening my life and alleviating the despondency caused by my unpopularity at Oxney's. Nevertheless, when I returned from one of these gatherings to plunge once more into an atmosphere of hostility and indifference, I had the depressing sensation of having left an artificial paradise for an unpleasant world of reality which might well, I believed, prove to be the more normal world of the two.

I was still in the hero-worshipping stage, though my form of worship had now become a little more sophisticated. Marston's influence on me was, for the moment, supreme. Oscar Wilde says that any influence is a bad influence which seems to be pushing a little too far the cult of individuality. The important thing is to know whether the influence is a good or bad one. I think that aesthetically Marston's influence was good. He improved my literary and artistic tastes and helped to demolish many of my false gods. On the other hand, he did a good deal to undermine my religious faith. He professed himself a militant agnostic, and he was apt to indulge in a blasphemy that was often of a Marlowesque coarseness. He had an extensive knowledge of the obscene passages in the Old Testament and would introduce embarrassing references to them into his Sunday Questions, and he had made a close study of religious dogma, scenting in it an admirable scope for humour. At first I was inclined to be shocked by his irreverence—for instance, when he had said that the Trinity put him in mind of a music-hall turn, the Father, the Son and the Performing Pigeon—but very soon I came to be amused by it and even sought to emulate him.

In any case, my faith had never been a very healthy one. In a diary of my mother's, written when I was five years old, I found the following passage: "He is most persistent in knowing the reason why and argues out every point, so that I hardly dare tell him any Bible story. When I do, he inclines to favour the wrong side, Adam and Eve, the Egyptians, and even Cain and Jezebel, and

he is always saying he thinks God must be very wicked."
Which seems to prove not only how dangerous it may be
for amateurs to expound the Scriptures, but that, at the
age of five, I already had a tendency to rationalism.

I think, however, that Marston was less responsible
for discouraging any latent talent I may have had for religion than my grandmother, Lady Bourchier. It was owing to the religious instruction that I had received at her
hands and to the Protestant gloom of Stackwell, the
house in which she lived, that the City of God came to be
invested, in my childish eyes, with the attributes of an
Evangelical Valhalla that could only be entered with the
greatest difficulty and discomfort, to find, when one got
there, that it was inhabited by people like my grandmother.

Nevertheless, when the time came for me to be confirmed, I made up my mind to devote myself to my prep-
aration for it with the same earnestness as that with
which I had prepared myself for the Eton entrance exam.
At the back of my mind there was a haunting suspicion
that the rebuffs with which I was so constantly meeting
in my daily life might possibly be due to my lack of religion, and I made a valiant effort to whip up a religious
fervour in my soul. But it was not so easy. Few of the
boys who were being prepared for Confirmation at the

same time as myself seemed to be very deeply impressed by the solemnity of the occasion. The discipline of the Confirmation class was considerably less strict than that of the division, and the room in which it was held was so hot and stuffy that I was reduced to a condition of stupor. I was once again disagreeably affected by the Catechism. It had repelled me when I was a child, and indeed the Catechism has always struck me as singularly unfortunate in its tone, presenting as it does the doctrines of Christianity in an irritating, governessy manner ("My good child, know this"; "Let me hear if thou canst say the Lord's Prayer") calculated to alienate any self-respecting young person. It is surprising that the Church should never have thought of having it revised.

Marston had supplied me with a list of questions which, he said, I should insist on having elucidated. Some of them I can remember. "Why did Christ sit on the right hand of God? Wouldn't it have been politer to have allowed his Mother, who was a lady and a very remarkable one, to have occupied that position?" "How can we fear God and love him at the same time? Haven't we been told that 'Perfect love casteth out fear'?" "When Christ descended into Hell, wasn't it rather decent of the Devil to admit him?" But the elderly clergyman who was preparing us was so kindly and amiable that I didn't wish to make a nuisance of myself and the questions remained unasked.

The Confirmation, when it took place, was a great affair. My mother came down to Eton for the occasion, and the impressiveness of the service in the Chapel, the imposing appearance of the Bishop who confirmed us, and the general odour of sanctity that prevailed, combined to inspire me with the belief that I had at last "got religion."

This happy state of grace, however, was of short duration. Confirmation had affected me in the same way as a play which has for the moment impressed one on account of the skill of the actors and the glamour of its setting, but in which a more sober reflection discovers unconvincing episodes and faults of construction. My doubts had been only temporarily corked up, as in a bottle. There they had continued to ferment until the cork was forced out and they came bubbling forth more effervescent than before. Decidedly I had no aptitude for religious faith and, in strange conjunction, Marston and my grandmother had been the Comic and the Tragic Muses of my infidelity. The doctrines of Christianity seemed to me to be admirable in their way, if a little contradictory, but the privilege of understanding the necessity for Divine Revelation was withheld from me. Marston had said that self-respect was a better guide for one's behaviour than God, and far more reliable. After my fictitious religious zeal had subsided, I was left with sentiments about religion that were very similar to those of my early years with regard to sex. In this world there was so much to excite pleasure, curiosity and fear that it seemed a useless effort of the imagination to concern oneself unduly with the Above and Beyond. It would be more practical, I thought, to shut the door on God and the Universe and concentrate on the things in my room.

When I spoke of these conclusions to Marston he congratulated me. "I think you're probably safe now," he said. "Religion is like measles. When once you've had it and got over it, it's unlikely you'll have it again."

# VIII

## *Marston*

### (CONTINUED)

❖

After my friendship with Marston had continued for nearly a year, I had the unlucky idea of asking him to stay with me during the Easter holidays. It was the first time I had invited any of my school friends to Althrey. My mother had often urged me to do so, as she thought it was bad for me to be without male companionship during the holidays. No sooner had Marston accepted the invitation than I began to wonder if, as the first sample of my Eton friends to be presented to my mother, I had chosen quite the right person. As the time grew nearer to his coming I was assailed by an ominous foreboding, which was increased when my mother enquired, "Does your friend Marston hunt?" "I don't know," I replied. "I expect he does." The idea of Marston on horseback exceeded the limits of the most fantastic imagination. I kept on assuring my mother that Marston was very clever, to the point of overdoing it, so that she ended by saying, "Not too clever, I hope."

I had prayed that Marston, in view of a visit to a strange house, might possibly have thought of doing something about his clothes and his general appearance, but when he arrived I saw that this had not occurred to him. In the conventional atmosphere of my home he looked more extraordinary than ever. Neither did he, in his conversation with my mother, attempt in any way to modify his opinions. He appeared almost to glory in his ignorance of country pursuits and was unsympathetic about dogs and horses. At Eton I had admired his uncompromising attitude, but in the home circle I was beginning to find it a little embarrassing. It was not long before I realized that my mother had taken a violent dislike to him. But for the moment she said nothing.

I had entreated Marston so earnestly to restrain himself on the subject of religion that, on this point, he actually did make a concession. He even went so far as to accompany my mother and myself to church on Sunday, but he remarked to me on the way back that it was pathetic to see a foolish old clergyman wallowing in a morass of doctrine he didn't understand and couldn't explain. My mother overheard, and said to him reprovingly, "Mr MacGill is an excellent man and he does a great deal of good work in the parish."

I forgot to warn Marston about my mother's admiration for Queen Victoria, and I was horrified when I heard him say at luncheon that she was a tiresome old woman who had only acquired importance from having lived so long. "In England," he said, "longevity is accounted one of the major virtues," and he went on to say that he feared the example of our beloved Queen might set an unfortunate fashion in politics and that future statesmen might take it into their heads to try and achieve popularity by living a long time and resembling old ladies.

That evening my mother came into my room as I was going to bed. It was a moment she generally chose to make an appeal to my better nature, and I guessed from the mingled tenderness and gravity of her expression what she was going to say.

"My dear boy," she began, "you know that I am always delighted to have any of your friends staying here. I had hoped that you would make a lot of nice friends at Eton, but I'm afraid that I can't say I think that your friend Marston is at all a nice boy. He is not the kind of boy I care for you to associate with. To begin with, he is so horribly untidy and dirty. It makes me quite ashamed before the servants to have anyone in the house who looks like that."

Marston was in the habit of defending himself against this charge by saying that many of the saints were notorious for their dirtiness. When I adopted the same humorous line of defence, my mother said, "Well, my dear, if he were a saint I should not so much object. But your friend Marston is very far from being a saint. Indeed, he doesn't even seem to me to be quite a gentleman."

Knowing that my mother thought that anyone who didn't hunt and shoot was automatically excluded from the category of gentlemen, I felt that it would be useless to argue with her on this point.

"He may not be a gentleman," I replied, "but he is a genius."

"A genius!" my mother exclaimed. "Being dirty and precocious doesn't make people geniuses. Edison, Herbert Spencer, Cecil Rhodes, they are geniuses. I don't see that your friend Marston has anything in common with them."

"There are different types of genius," I protested, "and even if he isn't one, I like him."

"That, my dear," replied my mother, "is just what I'm complaining about."

I remained silent. There seemed nothing more to be said.

"Surely, darling," my mother continued, "you must realize that you wouldn't care to take that boy into any decent society—to Arley, for instance, or to any of the neighbours' houses. By the way, I thought it better to put off Colonel Stokes, who was to have lunched here to-morrow."

For this at least I was thankful. Colonel Stokes was the sort of person who would have incited Marston to the worst extravagances.

"When you are older, dear," my mother went on, "you will understand my reasons for not wishing you to have friends like Marston. We all make mistaken friendships when we are young, but, please, darling, don't let it occur again."

She kissed me and went off, leaving me in a state of considerable agitation. I had put up a poor fight in defence of my friend. Yet what could I do? It seemed that the state of life unto which it had pleased God to call me was one into which it was hopeless to try and fit people like Marston, and, as long as I remained in it, the only thing to do was to acquiesce. But I had been disloyal to my friend and my conscience was racked by guilt. I felt myself in the position of a Victorian daughter forced by her parents to reject a beloved but detrimental suitor. I lay awake dreading the morrow. Now that my mother had told me how she regarded my guest, the situation was going to be intolerable. Every time Marston opened his mouth I should feel her eyes fixed on me, judging the results of her exhortation.

As a rule, Marston affected a deliberate disregard for an awkward situation, but in this instance, as it was emphasized by my mother's increasing chilliness, he appeared to understand the position as clearly as if he had overheard the conversation that had taken place in my bedroom. On the following afternoon he told me that he had received a letter from his guardian calling him away and would be reluctantly obliged to curtail his visit. "I'm afraid," he said to me as we drove to the station, "that your mother didn't like me very much."

Although I was a little ashamed of the part I had played in this episode, Marston himself had not come out of it unaffected, and I began to have doubts as to whether he were quite the paragon I had thought him. In the setting of a country house permeated with the spirit of simple virtues and conventional ideals, he had not appeared to his advantage. His personality, which in the cultured shade of the school Library had seemed so brilliant, in rural surroundings produced an effect that was a little meretricious. It had struck a jarring note, like one of the new-fangled motor-cars in country lanes where I had been accustomed to drive with my mother in a pony-cart. In the atmosphere of my home the influence of heredity and environment was still powerful enough to affect my point of view. My mother's opinions still retained for me a considerable prestige, and perhaps, after all, she was the best judge of what was right for me.

Home influences had won, and in consequence Marston had lost a good deal of his glamour. It was a tarnished image of him that I now had in my mind's eye, and when I saw him again on my return to Eton it failed to recover its former brilliance. Our meeting was fraught with embarrassment on both sides. We neither of us referred to his visit. If I had had the sense to talk the matter over with him, humour might have come to the rescue, but I felt that it was too difficult a situation for me to tackle.

I heard that he had entertained some of his friends with a mocking account of my home life supplemented with mimicry of my mother's conversation, and this I very much resented. However much we may ourselves laugh at our parents, we dislike hearing other people doing so, as it seems to involve ourselves, and I became still more firmly ranged on my mother's side.

I continued for a while to frequent the gatherings in the school Library, and I remained on good terms with Delmer and Wilson, but, although they couldn't fail to realize that relations between Marston and myself were strained, they neither of them made any attempt to ease the situation. Indeed, they never lost an opportunity of repeating to me the things that Marston had said about me—that I was a snob, that I had no guts and wasn't worth bothering about, and other acerbities of a similar nature. I came to the conclusion that it was undignified to try to keep up any further pretence of friendship with Marston, and the friendship ceased.

# IX

## *Wagner and Deniston*

❖

There now flowed between myself and my former idol

> *"a dreary sea;*
> *"but neither heat, nor frost, nor thunder,*
> *"Could wholly do away, I ween,*
> *"The marks of that which once had been."*

I had been under Marston's influence too much and too
long for the rupture of our friendship to leave me unscathed. I soon discovered that in losing Marston I had
lost many other things as well. I had gained under his
auspices a certain measure of self-assurance. I had come
to flatter myself that, even if I were no good at games, I
was at least intelligent and amusing enough to hold my
own among people who were not entirely obsessed by

sport and athletics. That such people were in a minority I well knew, but now that Marston was no longer at my side to reassure me, I was beset by a fearful doubt as to whether they might not perhaps be, as my mother would say, "the wrong people," if it were not, after all, the playing fields of Eton that really counted, that it was there that the battles of life were won. I had allowed myself to stray into paths of futile cleverness which led nowhere. I decided to try and pull myself together and take my character in hand.

There was a little book that was very popular at the time, called *A Day of my Life at Eton,* in which the hero, who had started as a "slacker," had ended by getting his Colours and becoming a pride to his house. I determined to emulate him. It was now the Summer Half, and I took up rowing with earnestness and perseverance. Whereas I had previously spent my spare time on the river in a picturesque backwater, sketching, reading, or idly observing the beauties of nature, I now devoted it to an intensive study of the technique of oarsmanship.

This gave me very little pleasure and failed even to produce the pleasant sense of complacency which is usually the reward of strenuous virtue. It merely resulted in palpitations and exhaustion. It was fortunate for me that my exertions led to nothing more serious, for I was unaware at the time that there was something a little wrong with my heart. When I complained about my symptoms to Mrs Elton she read me a poem by Christina Rossetti in which the poetess asks, "Does the road lead uphill all the way?" and answers in the affirmative. It was a very nice poem, I thought, but it failed to give me the encouragement Mrs Elton had hoped it might. She would perhaps have done better to have felt my pulse, but she knew I had taken up rowing seriously and, in accordance with the Eton tradition, she believed that if my character was all right, the body would take care of itself.

I continued to plod wearily along the uphill road. I took part in a sculling race in which I came in last, an ignominy that plunged me into the depths of depression and self-contempt. However, the blackest hour comes before the dawn, and at this point there entered into my life two new factors to raise once more my flagging spirits; one of them was Wagner, the other a boy called Deniston.

Deniston was about sixteen years of age, my senior by a few months but lower in the school. He was in everything the exact antithesis to Marston. He was extremely good-looking and neatly built, and he obviously took a good deal of trouble about his clothes. Although it was not easy to achieve much distinction with the common-place ingredients of Eton coats, collars and black ties, he contrived to look as smartly dressed as the most gorgeous member of "Pop." His light-brown hair was always carefully brushed and shone with brilliantine. He had a natural elegance, and even with all the mud of the football field on him he never looked anything but gracefully romantic. A bronzed complexion gave him the appearance of a sophisticated edition of Walt Whitman's "tan-faced prairie boy," and a slight cast in one of his grey eyes and a crooked smile added a curious attraction to the classical perfection of his face. His voice, which was low and husky, was more indicative of his character than his rather too soigné exterior. If all this had been accompanied by a brilliant intelligence it would have been altogether too much of a good thing. Luckily it was not. However, he was far from being a stupid boy. He had a certain amount of natural shrewdness and he possessed both sense and sensibility, added to which was a nonchalant charm of manner exercised with an apparent indifference as to whether he charmed or not. In spite of the cast and the crooked smile, he had an air of singular candour, of an almost childish innocence. Yet his reputation was by no means as spotless as his collars and his cuffs, and he was the object of a good deal of scandalous gossip.

Marston, notwithstanding his conversational lewdness, was at heart a rigid puritan, and he was wont to express in no moderate terms his distaste for "that sort of thing" and for Deniston and his friends. It was partly for this reason, and because Deniston moved in rather exalted circles, that although I had been attracted by his appearance I had made no attempt to seek his acquaintance.

That Summer Half, Deniston sat immediately opposite to me in Chapel and I was able to study him without appearing unduly to stare. He certainly was remarkably good-looking. His face stood out from the row of less distinguished physiognomies like the one good picture in a mediocre art gallery. I noticed that he attracted other glances than my own, and of this I fancied he was not unaware, for he affected the slightly self-conscious indifference of those who know themselves to be the "cynosure of neighbouring eyes."

One Sunday coming out of Chapel we found ourselves side by side amongst the throng of boys in the doorway. Deniston turned to me and said, "Come for a walk?" I was taken aback by the unexpectedness of the invitation and for a moment I could only stare at him in amazement. However, my acquiescence seemed to be taken for granted.

We walked through the Cloisters in the direction of

the playing fields. At first the conversation was inclined to drag. "I hope you're going to be amusing," Deniston said to me. "I've heard that you are."

"Do you like being amused?" I asked. "I find that so few people do, and it's a little discouraging."

"You're a friend of that chap Marston, aren't you?"

"Not so much as I used to be. In fact, I see very little of him nowadays."

"Well, I'm not surprised," said Deniston. "He really looks too awful. One couldn't be seen about with him."

After a moment's silence he added, "I'm told he's very clever and amusing. It's a pity he looks like that. That's the trouble with so many fellows of that type." There was a touch of wistfulness in his voice. It was a pity, I thought, that if he had a yearning for higher things it should be curbed by a too fastidious regard for appearances.

We passed over Sheep's Bridge and sat down on the river-bank.

"You're very unpopular in your house, aren't you?" Deniston suddenly asked me. I was a little disconcerted at his being in possession of this damaging information.

"They're a ghastly lot, the fellows at Oxney's," he went on, "and perhaps it's rather to your credit that you should be unpopular. However, there was one fellow there whom I liked quite a lot. A fellow called Faulkner. He was sacked."

Faulkner, whom I have already mentioned, had been one of the athletic stars of the house and his expulsion had come as a shock to everyone. I remembered vaguely having heard that Deniston had been among those concerned in the affair that had led to his downfall.

"Was it he who told you that I was unpopular?" I asked.

"No. But he said that you played the piano very well. I like music myself, though I don't know very much about it. I went to a Wagner opera when we were in Germany in the holidays. It was a bit long, but I enjoyed it quite a lot. Jolly scenery there was, too. Can you play Wagner?"

"No. I'm afraid I can't."

"Well, you'd better learn some and you can play it to me."

As we walked back through the playing fields I enquired of Deniston why, in that surprising fashion, he had asked me to go for a walk with him.

"I really don't know," he replied. "I never think very much about what I do. I always do things on the spur of the moment. It often gets one into trouble, but one has a better time."

As I sat alone in my room that evening, I pondered over this strange and rather delightful encounter. I wondered what sort of impression I had made, whether I had given satisfaction and whether the conversation by the river had laid the foundation of a new friendship, or whether the next time I met Deniston in the company of some of his grand friends I should be cut. I wondered if he were really as wicked as he was reputed to be. Envy or excess of piety is apt to lead schoolboys to be a little too eager to think the worst of one another. At the same time, I thought, I shouldn't wish him to be entirely innocent, a mere victim of slander. Vice, if practised by persons of prepossessing appearance, and not too flagrantly, has for most of us a certain charm. And Deniston's appearance and personality were attractive enough to excuse a good deal. I thought of him as he had sat that afternoon on the river-bank, outlined against the foliage of an overhanging willow, the sunlight striking upon him from the rippling water. I was sure that my mother would approve of my having a friend like Deniston. She would describe him as a "nice clean English boy." In this, I felt, there was a touch of irony, for Marston, with all his uncouthness and his iconoclastic utterances, more truly represented my mother's respectable ideals.

I was anxious to know more about Deniston, his antecedents, his home life, and I made tactful enquiries of such of my friends as I thought might be informed on the subject. I learned that his mother was a well-known "Society beauty," a very fashionable lady, and that she was in the Prince of Wales's set. It was even hinted—well, it appeared that her son, if his morals were not all they should have been, might perhaps be excused on hereditary grounds.

Deniston had spoken to me of Wagner. I knew nothing of Wagner except the Bridal March from *Lohengrin* played on an old musical box in my nursery. The music master at my private school had said that his music was nonsense, and my cousin Emily had been to a Wagner opera and had thought it very disagreeable. Apart from this, Wagner had never been discussed either at school or in the home circle.

It often happens that, when something new and unfamiliar crops up, one finds it immediately and constantly recurring, as if chance had taken the matter in hand and was bent on driving it home. The first thing that caught my eye when I went into Ingalton Drake's bookshop on the following morning was a little book called *A Synopsis of Wagner's Nibelungen Ring*. I can see it still—a slim white volume with red lettering. It was a matter-of-fact little work, written with no attempt at style or poetry, but its effect on me, when I began to read it, was like that of Chapman's *Homer* on Keats:

> *"Then felt I like some watcher of the skies*
> *When a new planet swims into his ken."*

My interest in music had been aroused in the first instance by the sight of musical notation on paper. I was attracted to it pictorially. Wagner I approached along the paths of literature. As I read on, a wonderful new world unfolded itself. I passed enraptured through the green waters of the Rhine, into the resounding caverns of the Nibelung, up the pine-clad mountain slopes, across the rainbow bridge to the glittering turrets of Valhalla. I thought that the music must be wonderful indeed if it at all corresponded to this enchanted world. But my enquiries about Wagner were less successful than those I had made about Deniston.

I asked Delmer, who sniffed and said, "Oh, Wagner! I imagine it's just the sort of music you might like," from which I inferred that Wagner was one of those composers who "couldn't write a decent fugue." Wilson was equally unhelpful. "I haven't got any of his music," he said. "He only writes operas." Neither had the artistic Mrs Elton anything to say on the subject, beyond that she had heard he was very highly thought of by certain people. Thus, for the moment, all that I had to go on was the fact, not devoid of encouraging implications, that my cousin Emily and the music master at Elmley didn't like Wagner, and that Deniston did.

A few days later, passing a music-shop in Windsor, I caught sight of a vocal score of the *Rhinegold* in the window. My heart gave a leap. So must Dante have felt when he saw Beatrice on the bridge in Florence, an incident portrayed in an engraving in Mrs Elton's room. I burst into the shop with such violence, and demanded the score in so agitated a voice, that the shopwoman looked for a moment as if she were about to call for help. Alas! It was twelve shillings—too much for my slender means. I was so crestfallen that the woman was moved to pity. Her expression softened.

"May I look at it?" I asked.

"Why, of course," she said, handing me the precious volume.

I turned over the pages feverishly. There they were, the Rhinemaidens swimming about in shimmering semi-quavers, Alberich clambering up from the depths of the Rhine to the accompaniment of syncopated quavers and rising arpeggios, the theft of the Gold, followed by a scurry of descending scales out of which emerged the majestic strains of the Valhalla motif.

The shopwoman interrupted my trance by waving before my eyes a small paper-bound volume. "We have also the libretto," she said. "That is only a shilling." I bought it—it was better than nothing—and left the shop, casting a yearning backward glance at the score, which was being replaced in the window.

I walked on into Windsor Park and, choosing a secluded spot, sat down on the grass and began to read.

*"The Rhinegold*
by
RICHARD WAGNER
English Translation by H. and F. Corder
PRELUDE AND FIRST SCENE

Greenish twilight, lighter above, darker below. The upper part of the scene is filled with moving water which restlessly streams from *L.* to *R.* Everywhere are steep points of rock jutting up from the depths and enclosing the whole stage; all the ground is broken up into a wild confusion of jagged pieces, so that there is no level place, while on all sides darkness indicates other deeper fissures."

I entered spell-bound into the Wagnerian world. Windsor Park, the massive Castle, Eton, the whole world of reality became engulfed in the mysterious depths of the Rhine. My enthusiasm was not damped by the absurdities of H. and F. Corder's* translation:

"*Alberich.* Spoilt were your sport if 'stonished I stand here still. Near to me dive then, a poor Niblung longs dearly to dally with you.
   *Woglinde.* He offers to join us.
   *Wellgunde.* Is it his joke?
   *Alberich.* Gladly I'd seek to encircle one of your waists, should you kindly descend.
   *Woglinde and Wellgunde.* The languishing calf. Let us accost him."

It was all pure poetry to me. I read on until I was recalled once more to reality by the chimes of a distant clock warning me that I must hurry if I wished to be back in time for Lock-up.

I read the text of the *Rhinegold* again and again until I almost knew it by heart, and accompanied it on the dining-

*H. and F. Corder's translation of the *Ring,* the standard translation of the time, with its pathetic attempts to preserve Wagner's alliterative style, is a masterpiece of unconscious humour.

room piano with an improvisation based on the memories of my brief glimpse at the score. Hitherto I had not thought very much about Opera, believing it to be concerned only with Italian gentlemen in doublets making love to ladies dressed like Mary Queen of Scots. Now that it had been revealed to me that it could include a world of forests and mountains peopled with Rhine-maidens, gnomes and gods, I was inspired with the idea of writing an opera myself. Disregarding my lack of musical knowledge, my complete ignorance of orchestration, I set about searching for an appropriate subject. Something out of Homer perhaps? But the Homeric gods and heroes seemed to me to savour a little too much of the class-room. The Arthurian Legend? I had read the *Idylls of the King*, and the characters seemed a little insipid in comparison with their Nordic counterparts. It wasn't going to be so easy to go one better than Wagner, and soon the ambitious project dissolved in the melancholy conclusion that, even if I had the capacity, I should not have the leisure, still less the encouragement to write an opera just at present.

Whenever I had time, I would make a pilgrimage to the music-shop in Windsor to look at the score of the *Rhinegold* in the window. I lacked the courage to ask if I might be allowed to examine it again, and had to content myself with gazing at it reverently through the plate-glass as though it were a sacred relic in a shrine. Although I hadn't much faith in the efficacy of prayer, I continued nevertheless to pray for its possession day and night. Suddenly one day there came an answer to my prayer in the unexpected shape of my father.

On returning to my house one morning in the interval between schools, I was told that my father was waiting for me in Mr Oxney's study. As he had never before visited me at school I feared at first that something dreadful had happened, that my mother was dead, that I had unconsciously committed some grave offence. It turned out, however, that he was merely paying me a friendly visit. Finding himself at a loose end in London, he had come down to see how I was getting on.

I had never seen my father in so amiable a mood. There was none of that morose detachment which, in the home circle, affected me so disagreeably, and his caustic wit, generally directed against my mother or myself, seemed now to be with me rather than against me.

I may say that it was perhaps the first time in my life that I had been alone with my father away from home. Devoted as I was to my mother, I discovered that, in circumstances like the present, when my father was in a genial mood, it was far more exciting to be in his company than in hers. In the household, in the hunting field, my mother was at her ease, but in her dealings with a world that was less familiar to her she was apt to be nervous and flurried. My father, on the other hand, inspired me with a sense of security. I felt that he would always be able to dominate every situation, that his presence in any difficulty would be reassuring. Besides, he was so elegant, so distinguished-looking, with his well-cut clothes and his little pointed beard, that I felt proud to be seen in his company. I was glad that the boys at Oxney's should realize that I had such a father.

As I was showing him round the Schools I noticed Deniston in the distance, standing near the entrance to the school yard. Since our encounter on the previous Sunday I had not seen him again. He had been absent from his customary place in Chapel, and I had been disturbed by the thought that he might possibly have gone too far and been sacked. However, it seemed more probable that he was merely ill. I knew that, until I saw him again, I should be in a state of suspense. It was like waiting for the result of an exam. Had I been passed or ploughed? Also, a great deal would depend on the circumstances in which our next meeting took place. Supposing he were to see me in the company of someone he considered undesirable! Now I was confident that the circumstances could not have been more auspicious. Attaching, as he appeared to do, so much importance to appearances, he could not fail to be favourably impressed by my father. I skilfully steered my father towards where Deniston was standing, and he came forward and greeted us with a smile. I introduced him, and after a brief, cordial conversation my father and I moved on. Deniston called after me, "Wait for me after Chapel tomorrow."

"Who was that boy?" my father enquired.

"His name is Deniston. Perhaps you know his mother. She's a famous beauty, I'm told."

"Deniston," my father repeated. "It must be Kitty Deniston's son. There's a likeness."

"She's a friend of the Prince of Wales," I added. My father laughed. "So that bit of scandal has reached Eton."

I could see that I had gone up in my father's estimation for having such smart friends.

As we passed a bric-à-brac shop in the High Street my father asked me if there was anything I wanted for my room—a picture, a piece of furniture? A wonderful opportunity flashed into my mind. "No. There wasn't anything I particularly wanted for my room—but there did happen to be a book." Fearing that my father might think it was an ordinary three-and-sixpenny novel, I hastily added, "But it's rather expensive."

"How expensive?"

"Well, it's twelve shillings."

"Good heavens!" my father exclaimed in mock horror. "I don't think I can afford that. But here's something towards it." He thrust a couple of sovereigns into my hand.

I was overwhelmed with gratitude. At the same time my conscience pricked me. Ought I to confess the nature of the book I wanted? If it had been my mother, I should have felt myself obliged to tell her that it was a musical score, and it would probably have been denied to me. But my father asked no questions, and I appreciated the advantages of having to deal with a parent whom I cared for less and whom I felt less compunction in deceiving.

Although the gratitude I felt towards my father at that moment knew no bounds, it required a good deal of self-control to conceal my impatience for his departure. I didn't want to go to the shop with him, as the nature of the gift would be disclosed. Now that it was so nearly in my hands I was beset by alarming thoughts. Supposing in the meantime somebody were to buy the precious score. It was no doubt the only one in the shop, and I should have to wait for days before another could be procured. I had already experienced too many eleventh-hour frustrations. However, all went well. Soon afterwards, my father returned to London with my benediction. The score had not been sold, and I hurried home hugging it to my breast. It had been a wonderful day. I had got the one thing I wanted more than anything in the world, and Deniston's friendship seemed also to be in the offing.

# X

## *Illness*

❖

Getting what one wants is not always, as has been said, a greater tragedy than not getting it. The possession of the *Rhinegold* score acted like a magic gift that had the power to transfigure my surroundings. I could now afford to disregard my unpopularity at Oxney's. As I sat unspoken to at meals, my thoughts wandered happily in a maze of Wagnerian legend. My ears, deaf to the chatter of my neighbours, were charmed by Wagnerian harmony, Mr Oxney was dispossessed by Wotan, O'Sullivan by Alberich, and the clinking of the cutlery by the anvils of the Nibelungen.

Every evening I played the *Rhinegold* on the dining-room piano, and occasionally Mrs Elton would come in to listen to it, the concerts with which I used to entertain the Library having long since ceased. She liked Wagner very much but she seemed less enthusiastic about the libretto. Her artistic ideals lay more in the direction of the Orient. "What a pity," she said, "that Wagner had not turned his attention to Omar Khayyam. What a wonderful opera he might have made out of the *Rubáiyát*."

I told her that Wagner at the end of his life had had the idea of writing an opera about Buddha, but had not lived to carry it out. "What a pity!" she said.

As for Deniston, the walk we took together on Sunday had the effect of confirming the friendship, and we were now seeing as much of one another as was possible for boys in different houses. Whenever he was not playing cricket, which he did a little too often from my point of view, we used to go for walks, bathe together or entertain each other in sock-shops. Nearly every evening we attended* Lock-up Parade, a ceremony that consisted in walking up and down the High Street just before Lock-up, shouting "Good night" at all the boys one knew.

Walking with Deniston I had occasion to admire the exalted nature of his acquaintances. He was greeted by nearly every member of "Pop," and he was often stopped and spoken to by the élite. I felt myself glowing with re-

*The custom has since, for various reasons, been abolished.

flected glory. I was particularly impressed, on one occasion, by his declining, rather coldly, an invitation to tea by a highly important youth, ennobled by every kind of athletic distinction. "He's rather common, you know," Deniston explained to me. "I don't think my mother would care for me to go to tea with him."

So Deniston's mother, too, imposed her social standards. They must be high indeed, I thought, if they excluded someone who was the possessor of more Colours than the rainbow. My own mother's objection to Marston seemed very paltry in comparison.

Much as I had valued Marston's friendship, there could be no doubt that Deniston's was affording me a far greater satisfaction. The two friendships had something of a symbolical significance, in that they represented the two worlds that have continued to fascinate me throughout my life, the world of scholarship and the world of fashion.

At that stage of my development the latter was predominant. Although Marston had dazzled me with his intellectual brilliance, Deniston appeared to me to glitter more attractively. He also inspired me with a greater sense of worldly security. His feet seemed to rest on firmer as well as on more agreeable soil. There was a background of social success, wealth and the favour of royalty. His was the world of leisure and enjoyment. In Marston's world there was a touch of asceticism. It was harder and more strenuous. A certain amount of effort and discipline was necessary to maintain oneself in it, while in Deniston's world one had merely to bask.

Happiness in my youth always had a rather relaxing effect on my sense of duty. When things were going badly for me there seemed to be an ever-present threat of human or divine wrath urging me to strenuous endeavour, whereas in times of prosperity I tended to disregard the threat and allowed myself to float resistlessly on the stream of my inclinations.

I abandoned my efforts to become a champion oarsman and felt all the better for it. I paid less attention to my work. I relapsed once more into my artistic delinquencies and started painting again. One afternoon Deniston accompanied me on one of my sketching expeditions on the river. He sat watching me painting with so riveted an attention that I suggested he should try his hand at it.

"No fear," he said. "I'm not artistic. And anyhow, I should never dream of trying to do anything I couldn't do well."

"How do you know you can't paint," I asked, "until you try?"

"I've no intention of trying," he cried almost peevishly. "Why on earth should I? I'm good at cricket. I'm better looking and better dressed than most people, and that's quite enough, I should have thought."

"That's all very well," I said, "but you can't go through life on cricket and looks."

He made no reply. I glanced at him as he lay gracefully in the prow of the boat, his sunburnt skin contrasting agreeably with the whiteness of his well-cut shirt, and I reflected that perhaps after all it might not be so bad a thing to go through life as an *objet d'art*, and I felt a little envious of him.

The prevailing atmosphere at Oxney's was inclined to be puritanical, and my friendship with Deniston was regarded as an additional bad mark against me. An anonymous letter, in which I recognized the clumsily disguised handwriting of O'Sullivan, informed me that if I continued to be seen going about with Deniston, Mr Oxney's attention would be drawn to the matter, and I found one day that, during my absence from my room, Deniston's photograph, which had adorned my mantelpiece, had been torn up and thrown into the grate. This determined me still further to flaunt him in the face of the enemy. Obtaining Mrs Elton's permission, I invited him to tea with me in my room. I knew that, for all his languid airs and exquisite clothes, he was fairly handy with his fists and would have no difficulty in dealing with any manifestation of hostility that might occur. Indeed, I rather hoped for an incident, but nothing happened beyond my getting black looks from a group of boys in the doorway as we entered the house together.

On the following day Mr Oxney called me into his study and spoke to me of the danger of making undesirable friendships. I reported the matter to Deniston, and the next time he saw O'Sullivan in the street he went up to him and knocked his hat off. The incident was witnessed by two or three members of "Pop," who laughed and cheered, thus completing O'Sullivan's humiliation.

For several days afterwards I went in fear of reprisals. I expected O'Sullivan to try and take some sort of vengeance on me after Lock-up when I was cut off from outside protection. But nothing happened. It is possible that O'Sullivan had respected the well-known admonition from Above and had left vengeance to the Lord, for shortly afterwards I was visited with a severe attack of rheumatic fever.

I awoke one morning with the most excruciating pains in all my joints. I could hardly move. Mrs Elton took my temperature, found it alarmingly high and sent for the doctor, who seemed gravely concerned by my condition. My mother was telegraphed for.

For over a week I continued to suffer the most appalling agony, which was intensified by the sweltering heat of my tiny room in those torrid days of July. Neither was it alleviated by the consolations Mrs Elton saw fit to proffer. She appeared to think it a good opportunity to deliver herself of her theories on the problem of pain. She assured me that suffering fortified the soul and brought us nearer to God. I thought that if my suffering were to bring me near enough to God to enable me to ask Him a question, I should enquire whether He really thought it necessary to inflict so much pain on one of His creatures, and what actually was gained by it. Nor could I understand in what way suffering fortified the soul. A stomach-ache brought on by overeating, a birching occasioned by misconduct, might act as an inducement to exercise restraint in future, but pain that did not appear to be the result of any deliberate sin or folly seemed to me to point no moral and adorn no tale. I began almost to dislike Mrs Elton. In a more Omar Khayyam spirit, she brought me a plate of strawberries, for which she was severely reprimanded by the doctor, who said that, in a case of acidity, nothing more unsuitable could have been thought of.

As soon as I was well enough to be moved, I was transported to cooler and more spacious quarters in Windsor. I was carried out of the house on a stretcher, through an inquisitive throng of spectators, and I felt that, for once in a way, I was making quite an impression. I looked anxiously to see if by any chance Deniston were among the crowd, but then I reflected that it would hardly have been characteristic of him to join a crowd to look at anything.

The rooms my mother had taken for me were in the high part of Windsor, in a quiet street leading to one of the gates of Windsor Park, of which one caught a glimpse at the end of a perspective of neat Georgian houses. It was a welcome change from my rabbit-hutch. As I lay on my bed in the cool, light room, looking through the window at the sunlit balconies and window-boxes of the houses opposite, I had the curious sensation of being somewhere abroad. As I had never been abroad, my ideas of what the Continent was like rested on a purely imaginary basis. A sense of distance—for Eton and school life seemed very distant now—the change from the rampageous noises prevalent at Oxney's to the quite different sounds of footsteps in the quiet street, an occasional passing carriage, or the cry of an itinerant vendor; the presence of a nurse in a white linen uniform; memories of *Lettres de mon Moulin* or some other French book I had read—all these things contributed to the impression I had of being in some French provincial town.

Now that I had entered into the stage of convalescence I began to discover that suffering brought in its train certain fortifications of the soul—which, however, were not exactly of the kind that Mrs Elton had intended. The fortifications were of an egotistical nature. One felt that one had gained in importance through having been a source of anxiety. Suffering had established a claim to consideration. People were now bent on making things as agreeable for one as possible. Even one's irritability and unreasonableness were condoned.

Mrs Elton came up very often to see me and would sit chatting with my mother at my bedside. It was with some dismay that I heard Mrs Elton telling my mother how much she had enjoyed my playing Wagner to her. However, my mother took the information so equably that I was emboldened to ask her if she had any objection to Mrs Elton sending me up the score of the *Rhinegold* I had left behind at Oxney's—"the one my father gave me," I thought it politic to add.

My mother looked surprised.

"Your father? When did he give it to you?"

"Oh, the other day," I replied casually, "when he was down here."

My mother had obviously not been aware of his visit to Eton.

"You don't mind my having it, do you?" I asked.

"No, of course not, darling. I want you to have anything that will make you happy."

I hardly dared to believe that this concession denoted a real change of heart with regard to my musical interests, and I wondered how long I could continue to presume on the privileges of an invalid.

I was beginning to think that it was very strange that Deniston had not yet come to see me. I had counted on his being the first of my friends to put in an appearance. Every time the door-bell rang and I heard the sound of footsteps on the stairs my heart leapt up, but doorbells rang, footsteps echoed, and there was always a disappointment. I knew that Deniston was not the ministering-angel type. Indeed, he had once said that he avoided people who were ill because he disliked hearing about their symptoms. I refused to believe that he could be applying this principle to me, and I thought of every possible excuse for his neglect. Perhaps he imagined that I had gone home. Perhaps he was ill himself or was too heavily involved in his beastly cricket to have time to come and see me. In any case, he might at least have given some sign of life. It would have been a simple matter to write to him, but *amour-propre* kept me from taking a step that might be construed as a reproof or a demand for attention.

Nearly all my friends came to see me, even Delmer and Wilson, with whom, just before my illness, I had had a slight altercation. With Delmer the quarrel had been on the subject of Wagner, and I had had a row with both of them about my friendship with Deniston. They came now in a conciliatory spirit, but before long the Wagner controversy broke out afresh. Delmer, noticing the *Rhinegold* by my bedside, began one of his anti-Wagner tirades. I felt too weak to argue with him. All I could find to say was that it was, after all, a matter of taste. "A matter of bad taste," Delmer retorted. "Wagner's music is essentially the kind of stuff that appeals to superficial amateurs."

I lay back on my pillow in speechless fury. Wilson, a little embarrassed by his friend's lack of consideration for an invalid, went to the window and looked out.

"Oh, lord," he exclaimed. "There's Deniston."

"Deniston?" I cried excitedly. Only my extreme feebleness prevented me from jumping out of bed and rushing to the window. At the same time, I thought that it was unfortunate that he should have chosen to come and see me just when Delmer and Wilson were there.

"He's gone into the house opposite," said Wilson, turning from the window.

"You might call to him," I said, "and tell him it's this house."

"I'll be damned if I do," Wilson replied ungraciously. "And if he's coming in here we may as well be off."

Delmer went to the window in his turn.

"He doesn't appear to be in a hurry," he said. "He seems to have settled down over the way. He's looking out of the window."

I was still convinced that Deniston was looking for me and that he was making enquiries of the occupant of the house opposite as to where I was to be found.

"There's somebody with him," Delmer went on. "It's that chap Faulkner who used to be in your house."

"He was sacked," said Wilson. "I don't think, if I'd been sacked, I should care to come back here."

"I expect they're up to no good," said Delmer, glancing maliciously at me through his spectacles.

By this time I was in such a state of nervous exasperation that I felt like screaming at my two visitors to take themselves off. That Deniston's visit to Windsor had not been on my account was disturbing enough. Still more so was the fact that his movements should be watched by Delmer and Wilson, and that they should also be the witnesses of my discomfiture.

"I don't know why you should imagine they're up to no good," I said to Delmer. "It's not very likely there'd be a brothel or a gambling hell in a street like this."

"It's just the sort of street where there would be," Delmer replied. "However, neither of those establishments is absolutely necessary for your friend Deniston to misbehave himself in."

Luckily, at this point the nurse came into the room and said that she thought my visitors had been with me quite long enough. As they left, Wilson, who was the kinder-hearted of the two, suggested going across the street and fetching Deniston for me. I begged him to do nothing of the sort.

After they had left I succeeded in working myself up into such a state of agitation that I lay awake most of the night. Fate, I thought, could hardly have devised a more malevolent series of coincidences with which to torture my imagination. I knew, of course, that Deniston had been a great friend of Faulkner's, and it was only natural that he should visit him when he was staying in Windsor. But the fact that Faulkner had been sacked seemed, in my fevered mind, to invest the matter with a somewhat sinister aspect. On the following morning I made enquiries about the house over the way and learned that it was a perfectly respectable private hotel. Later in the day I saw Faulkner leaving with a suitcase, and, although I watched continuously, Deniston did not reappear. I felt that it was now more than ever inadvisable for me to write to him, for in disclosing to him my whereabouts I might awake in him the suspicion that I had been spying upon him from my window, and the last thing I wished for was that our relationship should be disturbed by any touch of awkwardness.

The peace of my pleasant room and the quiet street had been shattered, and I was thankful when, after a few days, it was decided that I was well enough to be taken home to Althrey.

# XI

## *Bayreuth at Home*

❖

With the change of scene my spirits revived, and the cloud that had overshadowed my last days in Windsor began to lift. Space is often a more rapid healer than Time, and local grievances are luggage that one readily leaves behind. Although the Deniston affair still continued to rankle, in the congenial atmosphere of my home I was less inclined to brood over it.

My mother had put me in one of the guest-rooms at Althrey, larger and more elegantly furnished than my own. It faced south and the windows overlooked the garden. I had the impression of being a guest in my own home. I had my breakfast in bed, a privilege that I had always regarded as the height of luxury, and, being obliged to spend most of my time in bed, I lay poring over the *Rhinegold* score in a state of rapturous exaltation in which there mingled the un-Wagnerian elements of summer sunshine, the scent of jasmine and the twittering of swallows.

My mother seemed now quite favourably disposed towards my musical tendencies. My first serious illness had perhaps awakened in her a more indulgent tenderness. She may have come to the conclusion that Mr Gambril had a little exaggerated the danger of artistic pursuits. It was possible also that my *suppressio veri* in the matter of my father and the *Rhinegold* had had its effect. Anyhow she listened to my enthusiastic dissertations on Wagner and went so far as to order for me the score of the *Valkyrie,* which I found even more entrancing than the *Rhinegold.*

These were happy days. There was that wonderful sensation of regaining strength, that renascence of vitality that fills the mind with vague creative impulses, all the more delightful for not involving the labour of realization, for, whatever Charles Kingsley may have said, it is very agreeable to "dream noble things" and not to have to do them. There was one project, however, that I had had in my mind during the last days of my convalescence which I proceeded to carry out as soon as I was able to resume my normal mode of life. This was the construction of a miniature theatre in which to stage Wagnerian opera.

I remembered that in one of the cupboards at Althrey there was a derelict dolls' house that had formerly belonged to my mother. It was the very thing that was required. The façade had pillars on either side and was surmounted by a pediment. By removing the front and substituting a curtain on a roller I converted it into a very adequate theatre. As a theatre site I selected a lumber-room on the ground floor which was empty save for a few garden accessories, and as I felt it would be simpler to rely on daylight for my lighting effects, I placed the theatre in a bow window and, covering the window-panes with coloured gelatine and tissue paper, arranged blinds and shutters so that the light could be directed on to any part of the stage as required.

The *Rhinegold* was to be the subject of my first venture. Although the *Valkyrie* was perhaps more exciting dramatically, the *Rhinegold* offered a scope for more interesting variations of scenery. A yard or two of green gauze supplied by my mother's maid formed the backdrop for "The depths of the Rhine," and the "jagged rocks" were fashioned out of cardboard painted with water-colour. I purchased a number of small dolls at the village toy-shop. Three of them, adorned with flaxen hair and tails of silver paper, were transformed into Rhinemaidens. A fourth, wearing a pixy-hood and a beard, represented Alberich, who, on the end of a piece of wire, was made to clamber up the jagged rocks in a realistic style, while the Rhinemaidens, attached by threads of unequal length to a revolving wheel, swam round in rather jerky circles behind the gauze.

My attempts to reproduce the steam effects I had read of as one of the novel devices of the Bayreuth stage were not very successful, for when I poured boiling water into a trough concealed beneath the proscenium, the steam messed up the gauze and caused the tails of the Rhinemaidens to come unstuck. A more serious deficiency was that the performance would have to take place without music. Even if I had moved the piano to the lumberroom, which in any case my mother would not have permitted, I should have been too fully occupied by my functions of stage manager to be able to attend to anything else. The gramophone in those days was still in its scratchy infancy and had not risen above popular songs and military marches. Little did I dream that, some twenty years later, it would have been possible to accompany the action with actual records of the music.

Within a week I had completed the other scenes of the

*Rhinegold,* the "Cavern of the Nibelungs" and the "Open Space on the Mountain Height" with Valhalla and the Rainbow Bridge in the distance. Particularly pleasing was the moment when they appeared from behind a bank of cotton-wool clouds after a realistic thunder-storm contrived by the shaking of a sheet of tin-foil accompanied by flashes of lycopodium powder.

The first public performance took place in the presence of my mother and the servants. It went off very well except for a few minor mishaps, such as Fricka falling off the Rainbow Bridge and dangling head downwards, and Alberich getting entangled in the draperies of one of the Rhinemaidens and being whirled upwards in a sort of Nuptial Flight. However, I had heard that even at Covent Garden, in the early days of Wagnerian production, such contretemps had been known to occur.

# XII

# *A Snobbish Chapter*

❖

In the relationship between parents and children there comes a time when the myth of parental infallibility begins to fade. Into my formerly blind devotion to my mother there had crept an element of criticism. My affection for her was undiminished, but I had come to realize that, apart from our natural relationship, we had very little in common, and although I was touched by the tenderness she displayed towards her only child, I often wished that a little more account could be taken of the difference of our characters. I was inclined to resent her prescribing ambitions for me that I was unable and unwilling to fulfil. I knew that, on the whole, I had been a disappointment to her. On the hunting field I had most certainly failed. Indeed, it seemed unlikely that I should

⟋⟍ ◆ ⟋⟍

ever succeed in achieving distinction in any of the fields cultivated by my mother and my relations.

However, disillusionment was not confined to my mother's side alone. I also had my ambitions, and there was one in particular which, at the moment, was very much in my mind. I had long been aware that, above and beyond my own sphere, there existed a brilliant world of fashion. My interest in it had been intensified of late by my association with Deniston and others of his kind. My sober thoughts had learned to stray in the direction of these glittering Elysian fields.

There was a new illustrated weekly which I used occasionally to see, containing photographs of smartly dressed fashionable ladies. Another periodical, *The World*, gave accounts of the doings of the "Smart Set," chronicles of race-meetings, balls and fashionable parties. The goddesses and heroines of Greek Mythology, whom I had worshipped as a child in the drawings of Flaxman and the pictures of Lord Leighton, were now displaced by the figures of Lady Warwick, Lady de Grey, the Duchess of Sutherland and other "Leaders of Society."

Society! The word has changed its significance since the days of Wilde and Ouida. Now, no longer indicative of fashion and high birth, it has been democratized to the state of embracing all humanity and only suggests sociological treatises on the more earnest activities of the human race.

Hitherto I had taken for granted my mother's outward appearance and her social qualifications. Now I was beginning to realize that, whatever other excellent qualities she might possess, "smartness" was not one of them. As a child I used to think that she had every perfection. I even used to think that she was beautiful, just as I thought that Queen Victoria was beautiful, from a sense of loyalty and reverence. But as soon as I gained a maturer understanding of the nature of physical beauty, this delusion had ceased. Similarly, I had believed my mother to be exquisitely dressed, but now I knew that such elegance as she achieved was of a distinctly rural type and that her dresses were made by the local dressmaker.

My mother's field of action was essentially the country. In London she never seemed to be quite at her ease. At social gatherings, even in the country, she often appeared shy and embarrassed. I remember on one occasion at a garden party, when a *nouveau riche* neighbour, whose social pretensions had been unduly raised by the marriage of one of her daughters to a baronet, implied by her manner that she considered my mother to be of little importance, my mother failed to react in the way I felt she should have done. I wished that, in the social world, she could have displayed the same courage and dash that she did in the hunting field. In this new snobbish phase of mine it was a sorrow to me that my mother was not a "Society leader," or at least a member of the "Smart Set." If I was a disappointment to my mother, she was also a disappointment to me.

My father, on the other hand, was in this respect all that I could have wished him to be. I knew that he had a great many friends in fashionable circles. I had read in *The World* that he was a "*persona grata* at Court." But he never showed any inclination to bring either my mother or myself into contact with his smart friends. No doubt he thought we might prove an embarrassment to him in the *beau monde.* He was an ambitious man bent on succeeding in his career, and perhaps he feared that my mother's tactlessness—she often said rather tactless things out of nervousness—might prejudice his relations with influential people. Thus, although my mother continued to hold the first place in my affections, I had for my father a greater admiration and respect. I only wished he were more amenable.

Similarly, my newly acquired appreciation of social

distinction discovered a greater source of pride in my father's family than in my mother's, although I was less intimate with them and less fond of them. My father's family was a numerous one. He had eight brothers and three sisters. They did not appear to be so closely bound together by family affection as were my mother's brothers and sisters. However, in one thing they were united, and that was their hatred for my grandmother, Lady Bourchier. It was hardly surprising that they hated her. She was not the kind of woman to inspire affection, nor did she wish to. She brought them up with the utmost strictness and she was violent in her mode of chastisement. I was told by one of my aunts that she had once stood six of her children in a row and had administered to the first of the line so formidable a box on the ear that the whole lot of them had fallen over like ninepins.

The atmosphere of Evangelical gloom in which they had spent their childhood must have been appalling. They were allowed few enough diversions during the week, while the rigours of Sunday surpassed the wildest dreams of the Lord's Day Observance Society. All the pictures in the house except those of a religious character were turned with their faces to the wall. Anything in the nature of a toy or game was put away, and the hours not devoted to prayer were spent in study of the Scriptures.

As a result of their upbringing my uncles and aunts grew up to be worldly and irreligious, except for one of my uncles who became a clergyman; however, he contrived to get his own back on my grandmother by being extremely High Church.

If my grandmother had any worldly failing it was that she was inclined to attach a certain importance to the antiquity of her lineage, and if she failed to make her children religious, she at least inspired them with a sense of their social superiority, with which I in my turn was duly impressed.

# XIII

## Country Life

❖

My mother disliked hearing me complain that people bored me. She said that it was my own fault if they did, and she would speak to me of "sterling qualities" and the "salt of the earth." "A world composed exclusively of geniuses," she used to say, "would be insufferable." This was no doubt true, but it was nothing new to me in the way of an argument. It was the old trouble of the "common man." I couldn't help reflecting that, although a world composed of geniuses might be insufferable, I would, on the whole, have preferred it.

It seemed to me that among our neighbours at Althrey there was an unusually large percentage of people who could be classed as high-grade bores, and that life at home would have been more enjoyable if I hadn't

❦

been obliged to see so much of them. I naturally didn't think that I myself was a bore, but I had no doubt that a good many of my mother's friends thought that I was. In an environment exclusively devoted to sport I had little opportunity to shine.

I liked being in the country. I had a Wordsworthian enjoyment of nature, and in my childhood, when I could spend my time rambling in the woods, boating on the river or riding about the countryside without having to join in collective sport, I had been blissfully happy. But now that I was growing up I was obliged, and felt it my duty, to apply myself to the more manly occupations of hunting and shooting. Not that I was averse to either of them in moderation. But they were always too strenuously practised and they went on far too long.

It has been said that the English take their pleasures sadly. Not sadly, I used to think, but too persistently, and the pleasures of field-sports were considered not so much as pleasure as the fulfilment of some sort of sacred national duty. The long days of hunting and shooting against which it would have been criminal to protest were as irksome to me at home as were the organized games at school. I often quite enjoyed the first hour or so, especially on a fine morning when the landscape was veiled in autumnal haze and the dew-spangled hedge-rows glittered in the sunshine. But the contemplation of nature would too often be interrupted by the finding of a fox, which entailed galloping for miles and jumping the most terrifying fences, or by a rocketing pheasant which nine times out of ten I would miss, thereby covering myself with confusion.

I often used to envy the workers in the field who were exempt from this *"esclavage sportif."* The most arduous labours of agriculture, I used to think, would be preferable to the long-drawn-out amusements enforced on me by my social position. But I was obliged to bow in the house of Rimmon and pretend that I was enjoying myself.

In those days—at any rate, in my own milieu—young people were not encouraged to assert themselves unduly, and manifestations of opinion in any way departing from the normal were frowned upon by the middle-aged and elderly gentlemen who frequented my mother's house. Whenever my mother gave a dinner-party I used to dread the interval after dinner when the ladies had left the room and I had to sit diffidently listening to endless disquisitions on sport and politics—a state of affairs that

I found profoundly discouraging, and, in view of my Victorian belief in the permanency of institutions, I saw no reason why it shouldn't continue for the rest of my life.

Occasionally someone would take pity on me and try to draw me into the conversation, out of kindness of heart rather than from any interest in what I might have to say. Whenever this happened, I would be tongue-tied through shyness and the fear of exposing my ignorance, and was only able to mumble a few incoherent phrases. I longed for the self-confidence of a Marston that would enable me to electrify the company with some sensational remark.

Only on very rare occasions did I attempt impertinence, and then only when I felt that the objects of it were fair game. Once when that particularly fatuous friend of my mother's, Colonel Stokes, said to me, "Well, young man, what is your aim in life?" I replied, "Not to have to answer silly questions." But I felt that this sort of thing didn't really do me any good and it upset my mother.

If my attitude towards my elders and betters appears to be a little querulous, it must be remembered that I was going through the "awkward age," a period when one's outlook is liable to be distorted by self-consciousness. At least, I never adopted the pose of being "misunderstood." I had been permanently cured of that by a nauseating little book bearing that title which my mother had read to me as a child.

My only real friends in the neighbourhood were the Harveys, and this friendship was an ample compensation for any lack of sympathy I met with elsewhere. They had been at one time our nearest neighbours but had recently moved to Ellesmere, a picturesque little town about nine miles distant. Nine miles seemed a long way when one's only mode of locomotion was a bicycle, and the going was undoubtedly heavier on the bicycles of those days than it is on the modern machine. Also the road, like the road in the poem, was "uphill all the way." Indeed, it seemed to me to be uphill both ways. But such was my devotion that I used to make the journey twice and often three times a week in order to spend the afternoon with them.

Ellesmere lay just across the Welsh borders in Shropshire, a county which, harbouring, as it did, both the Harveys and Arley, where I had spent so many happy months of my childhood, had assumed in my mind something of a magic quality, and crossing the boundary line—the spot was indicated on a milestone—used to give me almost as romantic a thrill as when later in my life I approached the frontiers of Italy.

The Harvey family, consisting of Mrs Harvey and her two daughters, Lydia and Christina, lived in a pretty Regency house on the banks of the mere from which Ellesmere took its name. There was a Mr Harvey, but he seemed to be very rarely at home. Mrs Harvey, elegant in her clothes and witty in her conversation, was the nearest approach I had yet experienced to that world of fashion I dreamt of so longingly, and I was passionately devoted to Lydia and Christina. It would be hard to say of which I was the fonder. I was as happy, if not happier, in the company of both of them as I would have been with either of them singly. They seemed to complete one another. The two girls shared my youthful antipathy for bores, and I enjoyed in their company a pleasant sense of solidarity in the face of sterling qualities and the salt of the earth.

My mother often said that, if one really tried, one could always find something interesting in everybody. The Harveys went further than this, and had developed an amusing habit of deliberately dramatizing their neighbours, especially those who did not appear to possess any very dramatic characteristics. It had become a sort of game.

There was a Miss Crawford, an elderly spinster who lived in an ugly castellated house on the opposite side of the mere. She was very tall, gaunt and angular, and was afflicted with a permanent stoop and a melancholy air. Around this lady the Harveys had woven a legend that she had once been passionately in love with a midget and, owing to their disproportionate heights, had been obliged to stoop in order to receive his endearments. After some years of this unsatisfactory love-making the midget had deserted her for another midget. In proof of this sorrowful tale the Harveys insisted that, whenever Miss Crawford was obliged to bend down more than usual to pick a flower or to gather up something she had dropped, her eyes would fill with tears. "It is obvious," they said, "that the associations of stooping are painful to her."

I was occasionally taken to visit Miss Crawford, and whenever she made a remark that could be construed as referring to her unfortunate love-affair, we would exchange knowing glances. She said, one day, speaking of a particular kind of flower, that she preferred the dwarf variety, and another time she actually said that her favourite fairy-story was Tom Thumb. Poor woman, she was always playing into our hands. Our behaviour was hardly a charitable return for her hospitality, but she remained happily unaware of the tragic tale that had been attached to her and it afforded us a good deal of quiet fun.

Another butt of the Harveys was the Stanton family, who lived half-way between Ellesmere and Althrey. We had nicknamed them the Trappists for the reason that they very rarely spoke. They were friends of my mother and she would frequently take me to luncheon with them. I had been accustomed to look upon this as rather an ordeal until the Harveys invested the silence of the Stantons with the interest of a mystery problem and charged me with the task of discovering some sensational explanation of it.

I think that one of the reasons why my mother liked the Stantons was that she enjoyed talking, and in their company she was able to indulge in an uninterrupted monologue.

They lived in a house which, in normal circumstances, might have had quite a pleasant atmosphere. But years of accumulated silence seemed to be spread over the rooms like a funereal pall. This was particularly oppressive in the dining-room. However, luckily there was always a great deal to eat and this helped matters a little. My mother, seemingly unconscious of the encircling gloom, would keep up a lively monologue, but all the while I had a grim vision of meals when the family was alone, the silence relieved only by the sounds of mastication.

There were three sons. The eldest, Edward, was about my age. They were keen on sport, and my mother looked upon them as highly desirable companions for me. She was distressed at my not liking them better than I did. She said, by way of recommending them, that they had hearts of gold. Lead, I should have thought, would have been a more appropriate metal for her simile, and if there was anything golden about their silence, their habitual expression was one of sullen disdain. One day, when I was walking in the grounds with Edward, he handed me the gun he was carrying to shoot at a rabbit. I missed it, and the air of contemptuous resignation with which he took back the gun from me was more galling than any derisive comment could have been.

I sometimes wondered if the Stantons ever spoke with one another when they were alone. It was conceivable, I thought, that they had developed a faculty for communicating telepathically. When I mentioned this possibility to the Harveys they agreed that to witness a telepathic quarrel would be an interesting experience.

I forget what explanation was found to account for the

silence of the Stantons, but I am sure it was highly ingenious. Nor can I remember the circumstances relating to other neighbours who were subjected to this artificial infusion of interest. I found the system very helpful and was grateful to the Harveys for having invented it, but I refrained from speaking about it to my mother.

## XIV

## *The Bassetts*

———

## *Lady Bourchier's Visit*

❖

Our rector, Mr MacGill, had recently died, and at the beginning of the summer holidays a new clergyman, Mr Bassett, accompanied by his wife and a dog, had come to succeed him.

Mr Bassett was as unlike his predecessor as it was possible to be. Mr MacGill had been old, feeble of intellect and rather slovenly. He very rarely indulged in any form of social recreation and had confined his attentions to the poor rather than to the well-to-do. The Bassetts, on the other hand, were young, alert, of prepossessing appearance, and displayed a partiality for county society. Mr Bassett had been a curate in a fashionable London parish

⬥

and would, in his conversation, occasionally let drop some grand name or other. My mother was very favourably impressed by him. "It is nice," she said, "to have a clergyman who is a gentleman."

The Rectory, which in Mr MacGill's day had worn an air of poverty-stricken simplicity amounting almost to squalor, had been re-decorated in a highly tasteful manner, with gay wall-papers with roses on them and chintzes to match. The drawing-room was crowded with what-nots and occasional tables covered with china ornaments and photographs in silver frames. It is true that there were a good many objects about the place which could have been described, in the words of Henry James, as "gimcracks that might have been keepsakes for maid-servants and nondescript conveniences that might have been prizes for the blind." Nevertheless, I was so agreeably affected by the general air of artistic luxury that I thought, had I not been destined for a diplomatic career, I might have been well content to be a clergyman with such a nice house.

Mr Bassett was reputed to be very High Church. Certainly the services were a good deal brighter than those conducted by Mr MacGill. The majority of the parishioners paid but scant attention to the subtleties of ritual. Church for them was church, and as long as the clergyman was a decent fellow, they didn't care whether the altar frontals were changed with the seasons or whether there were six lights on the altar or sixty. In any case, I never heard any complaints about Mr Bassett, whereas in the days of Mr MacGill there had been frequent mutterings about the unintelligibility of his diction and the slovenliness of his attire.

Mrs Bassett was a plump, smiling, motherly sort of woman. Having no children, she found an outlet for her motherly instincts in a passionate fondness for her dog, a Skye terrier, whose extremities were so densely overgrown with hair that, until it moved, it was difficult to guess which was which. She said it understood every word she said. If that were the case, it must often have been a little nauseated by the baby-talk she lavished on it.

Both the Bassetts were interested in painting and music, and, although they couldn't in any way be compared with the Harveys, it was nice to have so near at hand people with whom I could talk about subjects that interested me.

Mrs Bassett painted in water-colours. The walls of the drawing-room were hung with examples of her art. She was particularly happy in her rendering of flower-gardens. She also played the piano well enough to be able to play duets, but she was apt to be so carried away by her emotions that it became difficult to keep time with her.

My mother, having to some extent raised the embargo on my artistic activities, appeared not to mind my indulging them in the company of Mrs Bassett. Besides playing duets with her, I used often to go out with her on sketching expeditions. There were a great many pretty "subjects" in the neighbourhood, especially along the banks of the river Dee. At that time my great passion was for Turner. Turner was in painting what Wagner was for me in music. I hankered after compositions that were more violently picturesque than those provided by the placidly flowing Dee, with its low grassy banks, the domesticated pasture lands and the mild outlines of the distant hills. I longed for something more in the nature of the castellated Rhine, the hill towns of Italy, the Swiss lakes and Alpine passes. The nearest approach to a Turneresque view I could find was the Roman bridge at Bangor-is-y coed, about half a mile from Althrey, with a background composed of the church tower, a clump of elms and the straggling village.

Mrs Bassett didn't like painting architecture unless it took the form of a thatched cottage with roses clustering on the porch. Her ideals in art seemed to me to verge on the pusillanimous, and I cannot say that she exerted much influence on my aesthetic development, except in the minor point of enriching my palette with a new colour called green oxide of chromium. I was liable in my painting to be obsessed by a particular colour, just as a musician, in his first orchestral efforts, often pins his faith to some orchestral timbre, harp, muted brass or xylophone. I used to imagine that the use of primrose aureolin, rose madder or alizarin crimson might enable me to achieve a masterpiece. Now, for a while, I continued to see things, not in a rosy light, but in a haze of green oxide of chromium. However, I soon came to the conclusion that the colour was more suitable for Mrs Bassett's horticultural studies than for my Turneresque visions, and I abandoned it to return to a more prismatic range.

Towards the end of the holidays this period of art and culture was interrupted by a visit from my grandmother, Lady Bourchier. My mother had invited her to stay at Althrey, never for a moment believing that she would come, as she had hardly ever been known to displace herself. To my mother's consternation, the invitation was accepted.

We wondered if it would be necessary to turn the pictures with their faces to the wall on Sunday and whether it would be advisable to revive family prayers, a rite that had been abolished some years ago. My mother decided that this would savour of hypocrisy, and luckily my grandmother announced that her visitation would not include Sunday. The only precaution that my mother took was to remove from the drawing-room a copy of a Raphael Madonna which she feared might possibly give offence.

I was less apprehensive than my mother. Indeed, I even looked forward to my grandmother's visit as an exciting experience. I had never seen her outside her usual environment, and I wondered if, during her short stay, she would succeed in imposing on Althrey the dank miasma of Calvinism that prevailed at Stackwell. My mother wondered how she could best be entertained. I suggested taking her over to luncheon with the Stantons. It would be interesting, I thought, to observe the contrast of two different kinds of gloom. My mother, less experimentally disposed, didn't favour the idea. In ordinary circumstances it might have been a good thing to invite the local clergyman to meet her, but Mr Bassett was far too High Church and my grandmother would have been outraged by his views. In the end, we came to the conclusion that absence of entertainment, beyond a few quiet drives about the countryside, would be the best solution.

When eventually my grandmother arrived, she was noticeably anxious to make herself as agreeable as possible. She pronounced Althrey to be a "nice little place" and commented favourably on the extent of the view. But, in spite of her condescending appreciation of everything and an unusual expansion of her rather grim smile, she was unable entirely to divest herself of her forbidding manner and her inquisitorial air. One was continually on tenterhooks lest she should discover some book or picture or some form of laxity in domestic matters that might excite her condemnation. She had a way of regarding even inanimate objects as if she suspected them of being about to do something dreadful.

In the mornings, when my mother was occupied with household affairs, the entertainment of our guest was left to me. I have spoken in a previous volume of my grandmother's interest in bird-life. Apart from religion it was the only interest she had, and although my own passion for ornithology had somewhat diminished in the last few years, I revived it for the purposes of amusing her. I took her to see a spot where a long-tailed titmouse had nested that year and pointed out to her the fragments of moss and lichen still clinging to the branches. Remembering that nut-hatches had always been her especial favourites, I showed her a hole in a tree where a pair of nut-hatches had reared their family. I took her down to the river in the hopes of seeing a kingfisher, but there was not a kingfisher to be seen. Although these expeditions had something of a negative quality, they seemed to please my grandmother, and at any rate kept her occupied. She was less interested in the various beauty spots I showed her. I don't think she cared very much about the beauties of nature. She seemed to think that they were not there to be admired but to inculcate some moral lesson, and that appreciation even of the works of God partook a little too much of sensual pleasure.

My grandmother, walking in the country lanes, was a strange and alarming spectacle, and the yokels stopped and stared. Attired in a black shawl over a tight black bodice punctuated with buttons of jet, a long black silk skirt with the hint of a bustle, and a black coal-scuttle bonnet which had the effect of concentrating the menacing expression of her features, she looked like Savonarola masquerading as Betsy Trotwood.

I remembered that as a child I used to believe that there were pulleys concealed beneath her skirts by which she raised them off the ground when she went out walking, but she must have given up the device, for now she allowed them to trail, irrespective of dust or mud, and the best part of her maid's time must have been spent in brushing and scrubbing. Perhaps it was done deliberately in order to inflict a penance on her, for my grandmother believed in inflicting penances.

These ornithological outings had the result of somewhat diminishing the fear with which Lady Bourchier had always inspired me. She seemed at moments to be almost human. But I doubted whether it would be possible ever to feel completely at one's ease with her. The steel-like quality of her mind, together with the narrowness of the limits within which it worked, gave the impression of a kind of trap in which, at any moment, one might be caught.

Although she must have deplored the absence of family prayers, she made no comment on the subject. But every evening after dinner she would take up her Bible and read aloud to my mother and myself for what seemed an interminable period. The passages she read appeared to have been selected at random, for many of them, such as the Sealing of the Tribes and the Genealogies, were devoid of spiritual edification, and once or twice she was obliged to skip certain parts which, thanks to Marston's researches, I was able to identify. Perhaps she had left the choice of her readings to the Author of the work and had trusted to Him not to let her down.

Occasionally she would invite me to play hymn-tunes

to her. She did not seem to care for my attempts to clothe them in Wagnerian harmonies, and when I played her "Onward, Christian soldiers" in the minor key and asked her if she didn't think it sounded nice like that, she replied rather dryly, "I think I prefer it as it was originally written."

Like so many things dreaded in advance, my grandmother's visit had turned out to be a good deal less formidable than we had feared it was going to be. I was compelled to readjust my opinion of my two grandmothers. Mrs Farmer, my maternal grandmother, had the temperament of an angel, but, as might be expected of such a temperament, she was a little lacking in character. Lady Bourchier was decidedly the more interesting of the two. I didn't flatter myself that Lady Bourchier was in the least fond of me. It would have been unreasonable, as Spinoza says of God, to expect that, even if I had loved her, she should love me in return. But at least she was no less fond of me than she was of her other grandchildren, whereas Mrs Farmer had her favourites, and she shared the views of the rest of the family about art and sport, which to Lady Bourchier were matters of complete indifference. There was another point that, in my eyes, weighed a little in Lady Bourchier's favour. She was a Baroness in her own right.

I couldn't help thinking that the success, such as it was, that had attended my grandmother's visit had been largely due to the exertion of my own personal charms. I was encouraged by the reflection that, in spite of the indifference and the rebuffs I so frequently encountered, I was gifted nevertheless with the latent powers of a lion-tamer or a snake-charmer.

The experiences of the summer holidays had, on the whole, contributed to raise a little my self-esteem. However, I feared that it might be lowered again pretty considerably when I returned to Eton. The apprehension I always felt when about to face once more the unsympathetic crowd at Oxney's was this time complicated by the problem of Deniston. I had never quite succeeded in banishing from my mind the bitterness inspired by his neglect of me during my illness, and now, as the end of the holidays drew near, it began once more to dominate my thoughts. The painful ending of my friendship with Longworth still rankled in my memory, and I felt that, if I were to find when I got back to Eton that I had been dropped by Deniston, the recurrence of this particular form of mortification would be more than I could bear, and that it would brand me for ever with the Cain-mark of social failure.

# XV

## *Happy Return*

❖

When I got back to Oxney's I found that I had been given another room of more ample proportions and less like a rabbit-hutch than my former habitation. It was on the first floor and looked out on the same courtyard, so that I still had before my window the plane tree for which I had come to cherish a pantheistic fondness. The new room had the advantage of being more easily accessible from the entrance door, and I foresaw that I should be less exposed to hostile encounters in the passages. I also discovered that my arch-enemy, O'Sullivan, had left. I was not told the reason for his departure, but I knew that, as Wordsworth said of the death of Lucy, this was going to make a "difference to me."

My spirits rose as I contemplated the amenities of my new quarters. Things were beginning well, it seemed—

⌒◆⌒

two of the boys had actually spoken to me and enquired after my health. I wondered whether these things might be good omens, presaging a favourable turn in my affairs. However, it still remained to be seen how matters stood with regard to Deniston. It would be quite in keeping, I thought, with the capriciousness of Providence that I should now be dealt a back-hander after having been patted on the back.

Luckily I was not left very long in suspense. That same afternoon I came upon him in the High Street. He greeted me with a friendly smile, and it was at once evident from the conversation which ensued that nothing was altered in the state of our friendship. The only thing that struck me as a little peculiar was that he made no mention of my illness. Although I should have very much liked to know the reason for his behaviour, I refrained from referring to it myself. I had sufficient worldly wisdom to know that, in matters of friendship, it is best to let bygones be bygones and, above all, to avoid recrimination.

It was in a cheerful mood that I returned to my house to confront whatever there might be in the way of unpleasantness. But at supper that evening I fancied that I noticed signs of a relaxation of the negative attitude usually adopted towards me by my house-mates. That this impression was not merely due to optimistic imagination other and more palpable indications came to prove. During the following days it became more and more obvious that a change of feeling had taken place. Boys no longer edged away from me at meals or cut me when I passed them on the stairways or in the passages.

It was, no doubt, my illness that had brought about this lifting of the ban. Next to the death of parents, a serious illness tends, in school life, to excite a greater sense of sympathy than any other pathetic condition. The spectacular effect of my having been carried out of the house on a stretcher and my return, as it were, from the jaws of death, had aroused a kindly interest, and a dispensation from playing football further emphasized my condition of invalidism and perhaps seemed to excuse in retrospect my lack of heartiness in the matter of games.

MacBean alone maintained an attitude of disapproval, but this didn't worry me very much. He had never been popular in the house, and now, deprived of the support of his ally, he grew steadily more unpopular, until finally he sank almost to the status I had formerly occupied. I was too well satisfied with this turning of the tables to indulge in any very melancholy reflections on the mutability of public opinion in Eton houses.

That I now enjoyed a certain amount of favour in my

( 155 )

house did not lead me to alter the opinion I had originally formed about its inmates. The fact that they were more kindly disposed towards me didn't seem to make them any the more interesting. I was sure that no other house at Eton contained so dreary a collection of boys—they might, one and all, have been the progeny of Mr Oxney himself—and there was not one amongst them of whom I felt that I wanted to make a friend. At the risk of incurring a return of unpopularity I was determined to preserve a certain aloofness. Luckily, owing to the isolated position of my room, I was able to do so without attracting undue attention, and I could spend the time after Lock-up alone in my room reading, or playing Wagner on the dining-room piano. I now delighted in these solitary winter evenings, for there was a difference between enforced solitude and solitude that depended on my own volition.

Now that I was at peace with my house, now that everything seemed to be going well with me, I began to enjoy a period of happiness which, if it was not the happiest time of my life, was certainly the happiest of my schooldays. At moments I felt almost uneasy about it and wondered whether, like Polycrates and his ring, I ought not to throw my Wagner scores into the Thames.

Not the least contribution to my well-being was the

dispensation from football which, incidentally, enabled me to see more of Deniston than had been possible during the cricket season. He was not particularly keen on the game, and although at Eton football was compulsory for all, he displayed his usual contempt for rules and conventions and took an afternoon off whenever it suited him. Many a half-holiday afternoon we used to spend in going for "runs," which, as far as we were concerned, meant sauntering about the countryside in shorts and sweaters. The memory of those expeditions, wandering in Deniston's company through the fields beyond Arches, and along the river-banks in the grey light of winter afternoons, evokes in my mind even today a sense of romantic nostalgia. There was certainly in Deniston's conversation nothing of Marston's wit and brilliance, but love and admiration can always supply any quality that we may desire. I think of the eloquent passage in *Coningsby*: "At school, friendship is a passion. It entrances the being, it tears the soul. All loves of after-life can never bring its rapture. . . . What tenderness and what devotion, what insane sensitiveness, and what frantic sensibility, what earthquakes of the heart and whirlwinds of the soul are confined in that simple phrase, a schoolboy's friendship."

But such friendships are apt to be precarious and

ephemeral. Their very intensity is a danger to permanence. One has heard of lifelong friendships that have begun in early youth, but it seems to me now that perennial alliances of this kind are only possible between those whose characters never develop to any great extent, or who remain throughout their lives under the spell of youthful associations, and that real and lasting friendships can only be made when our characters are more or less formed and when we have become our own masters. The friendships of youth are all too prone to fade through divergence of character and the divergence of ways.

# XVI

## *Pantomime*

❖

There was a boy in my division called Bartlett. He was generally known as Tartlet, although there was nothing in either his appearance or in his conduct to justify the nickname. He was strangely ugly. He had a small, narrow face and a prominent beak-like nose that was surmounted by enormous goggles. In stature he was under-sized, of decidedly skimpy proportions. The general effect was that of a shrimp with spectacles. However, this unprepossessing exterior concealed a highly artistic soul, and on the strength of this I made friends with him.

Bartlett had a habit of expressing himself in high-sounding phrases, and as his air was one of permanent seriousness, I assumed that he was immensely clever. Owing to this combination of earnestness and absurdity he was liable to be ragged. Consequently, he was rather on the defensive and did not respond to my advances until he had convinced himself that I was worthy of his confidence.

It appeared that he had made a study of the Drama in its more serious aspects, and I was a little surprised when he asked me if I was interested in Pantomime. As I had hitherto associated Pantomime with such subjects as Puss in Boots and Cinderella, this seemed to me a bit of a come-down. However, the Pantomime to which he was referring turned out to be a very different thing altogether. It was, so he explained to me, an Art-form in which the most transcendental themes might be expressed. "It may be defined," he said, "as organized emotional gesture."

I said that I remembered having once seen something of the sort in London. "L'Enfant Prodigue"—wasn't that a Pantomime?

He replied contemptuously that "L'Enfant Prodigue" bore the same relation to serious Pantomime as did musical comedy to Wagnerian opera. I was anxious to know more about this elevated art-form.

"If you're sincerely interested," he said, "I might perhaps be able to give you some idea of it. I have composed Pantomimes myself, and I occasionally perform them at home in private. But the difficulty of giving you a demonstration here is that it requires a musical accompaniment. At home my sister accompanies me on the piano."

"Well," I said, "I can play the piano."

He looked a little doubtful. "To accompany Pantomime is not at all easy, you know. My sister is a very good musician."

I continued to protest my adequacy.

"Very well," he conceded. "There can be no harm in trying it out. I will give you a couple of scenarios so that you may have some idea of the music required. I should suggest your taking passages from the Symphonies of Beethoven or Brahms and arranging them to suit the action. My sister always accompanies me with Beethoven or Brahms."

As I was not sufficiently familiar with the Symphonies of Beethoven and Brahms, I decided to resort to an improvisation of my own, and I spent the evening composing music for the scenarios he had given me on the dining-room piano.

Their titles were impressive. One was called "The Soul of Man in Conflict with the Universe"; the other, "Ideal Beauty emerging from the Chrysalis of Materialism." There were elaborate instructions for the musical accompaniment in the margin. "Two minutes of flowing music expressive of mysterious yearning. Sudden crescendo.

Procession of solemn chords," and so on, leading to a "triumphal march indicating exultation and victory."

On the following afternoon we met in one of the division-rooms in which there was a piano. Bartlett's manner was ceremonious and grave, like that of a doctor before an operation. "Of course," he said to me, "what you're going to see will necessarily be very incomplete. I can only show you the movements of the principal figures and shall confine myself to explaining to you the action of the supporting Chorus."

I was a little nervous as I sat down at the piano, and prayed that there might be no interruptions from outside. However, as it was a half-holiday afternoon it was unlikely that anyone would come into the division-room. I began to play the "Two minutes of flowing music" which I had conceived in the manner of the opening of the *Rhinegold*. Bartlett assumed a crouching position at the far end of the room. "Now," he called to me, "Crescendo, please." He rose suddenly to his feet and struck an attitude of defiance. Then he advanced to the centre of the room and began to revolve rapidly, launching out defiant gestures in every direction. After this had gone on for some time he returned once more to his crouching position. "At this point," he said, "a female dancer appears and does a dance expressive of encouragement, while the Chorus, who have entered, group themselves around in attitudes of despondency." He then resumed the role of the principal figure and went through a series of violent motions suggestive of shadow-boxing. He had removed his spectacles, and although he was very short-sighted, he displayed a remarkable skill in avoiding obstacles. Only on one occasion did he nearly trip over a form. The Pantomime continued for some time in alternating action between the protagonist and the Chorus. There was another dance by the female dancer, expressing a higher degree of encouragement. Bartlett's gestures became more and more violent and one began to feel that the Universe was definitely going to get the worst of it. "Finally," he explained to me in a panting voice, "the principal figure is borne out in triumph by the Chorus. This climax is most solemn and impressive. It is a pity I can't give you an adequate idea of it. You must try and visualize it in your mind's eye."

The second Pantomime, "Ideal Beauty emerging from the Chrysalis of Materialism," was a little similar to the first. There was less of the Chorus, and Bartlett's movements were more sinuous and feminine in character. "You must imagine," he said, "that the part is taken by a beautiful woman."

Strangely enough, I was able to imagine it. At that

moment I could have imagined almost anything. I had been so intent on my musical improvisation, so impressed by Bartlett's utter lack of self-consciousness, that my sense of humour had been completely knocked out and I was able to disregard the absurdity of his physique and see only the beauty of the idea. "You know," Bartlett said to me, "you seem to have a real talent for Pantomime music."

From that moment I became an ardent devotee of Pantomime. I was proud to be "in on it." I believed that in the composition of Pantomime music I had found my true vocation. I thought that it would be wonderful if Bartlett and I could enter into partnership, like Gilbert and Sullivan. Perhaps we could meet in the holidays with a view to furthering our collaboration.

In those days, before I had succeeded in controlling my proselytizing instinct, I was never able to be enthusiastic about anything without wishing to communicate my enthusiasm to others. The fact that Deniston liked Wagner made me think that he might perhaps like Pantomime also, and I persuaded Bartlett to give a demonstration for Deniston's benefit. I thought it advisable, however, to ask Bartlett not to give him anything too transcendental to start with. Bartlett was pleased with the idea of gaining so important a recruit for the cause of Pantomime and he was willing to make any concession. "Certainly," he said. "I will do 'The Fairy who longed for a Soul.' That is quite a light one."

As Deniston and I entered the division-room, where we found Bartlett waiting for us, I noticed that Deniston seemed a little taken aback by Bartlett's appearance, about which I had neglected to warn him, and from the moment I began to play the Fairy music and Bartlett set about expressing the Fairy's longing for a soul by a series of sweeping upward movements I realized that the experiment was doomed to failure. Deniston kept on interrupting with facetious interrogations, "What's she supposed to be doing? Winding up her watch?" "What's the matter with her now? Does she think she's going to have a baby?" until at last Bartlett broke off the performance, gave me a furious glance and flounced out of the room.

"Your little friend," Deniston remarked, "is quite ridiculous."

"You would have liked it," I said, "if he had been better looking."

"It certainly might have been less painful," he retorted.

I was annoyed with him for not having made any effort to take Pantomime seriously. At the same time I felt that it had been unreasonable to expect him to share my faculty for disassociating the beauty of the idea from the shortcomings of the performer. In any case, I was not going to quarrel with him about it, and my own faith in Pantomime had been a little shaken. In the light of a returning sense of humour I was forced to admit to myself that Bartlett really was rather ridiculous. I knew, of course, that great artists had been scorned and derided at the outset of their careers—Wagner for instance—but it didn't seem to me that Bartlett had the right kind of personality to carry anything through in the face of scorn and derision. I began to wonder whether I had not made a mistake in thinking that Pantomime was an improvement on Wagnerian opera. In the end the outcome of the aesthetic struggle in my soul was settled by Bartlett himself. He never forgave me for what, after all, had been a genuine, if misguided, effort to further the cause of Pantomime, and our relations were broken off.

After leaving Eton I completely lost sight of Bartlett, and I never heard of his making a name for himself in the world of art. However, I was reminded of him when, many years later, I saw some of the productions of the Central European School of Dancing, of which he seemed to have been to some extent a precursor—and I felt that I had perhaps been justified in my defection.

# XVII

## *Vale*

❖

As a result of getting caught in a rain-storm during one of my outings with Deniston and of sitting thereafter in damp clothes, I was laid up with a chill and a return of rheumatic pains. My illness was a slight one, but in my letters to my mother I gave her a rather exaggerated account of it, thinking it might be a good thing to emphasize the delicate state of my health and preserve for as long as possible the condition of invalidism that had procured me so many advantages. I little foresaw the consequences my deception was going to have.

My mother worked herself up into a panic, and having become obsessed by the idea that Eton was too unhealthy a place for a boy of my frail constitution, she wrote to Mr Oxney that she wished to remove me at the end of the Half.

❖

Ignorant of this decision, I went one morning into Mrs Elton's room and was a little dismayed when she greeted me with the compassionate mien of one about to break bad news.

"I am very distressed," she said, "to hear that we are going to lose you."

So sorrowfully did she regard me that, for a moment, I thought that she was implying that my days were numbered, that the doctor, in his diagnosis, had discovered some fatal seed of dissolution. When I realized that by "losing me" she meant not through my departure from the world, but from Eton, I was hardly less disturbed. For a time I refused to believe that there had not been some misunderstanding, but soon afterwards Mr Oxney sent for me and confirmed the news. He seemed less affected than Mrs Elton by the prospect of my leaving. He said he thought it was a great mistake that I should be taken away from Eton so early, but I gathered that he was not going to make any attempt to protest against it. "I never interfere," he said, "with the wishes of parents."

A year ago I might have welcomed the idea of leaving, but now, just as I had emerged from my social troubles and was beginning to enjoy my life at Eton to the full, it seemed singularly hard that I should be removed from it. I wrote to my mother imploring her to reconsider her decision, but my mother, like many people of vacillating character, once having made up her mind, had entrenched herself in adamantine obduracy. I suggested to her that my father, who was at that time on his ship somewhere in the Mediterranean, might not wish me to leave Eton, but it was a false move and only seemed to add to her determination.

Experience had proved to me the hopelessness of trying to revolt against the plans arranged for me by my pastors and masters, and an optimistic temperament disposed me to make the best of them. My mother had decided that, on leaving Eton, I was to go to France and complete my education there. In view of the diplomatic examination, she thought it advisable that I should acquire as soon as possible a sound knowledge of the French language, which I did not appear to be getting at Eton. The gloom into which the thought of leaving Eton had plunged me was somewhat relieved by the prospect of going abroad.

Ever since my early childhood I had conceived the most romantic visions of "abroad." My impressions had been gathered, in the first instance, from the scrap-screen in the drawing-room at Arley, on which views of foreign landscapes and towns were framed in garlands of exotic flowers and flights of brightly coloured tropical birds. Although later on I came to realize that these fascinating juxtapositions had been due to the ingenuity of my mother and my aunts who had made the screen, that humming-birds were not to be found in the neighbourhood of Geneva, that parakeets did not usually perch on the spires of Cologne Cathedral, I still continued in my subconscious mind to associate the Continent with these exotic additions and to imagine that "abroad" was a happy fantastic place, more exciting, more highly coloured than an environment with which familiarity had bred, if not contempt, at least at times a certain restlessness.

Literature had also fed my imagination. From Grimm and Perrault I learned that the happenings of fairy-stories took place in foreign climes. The books of Jules Verne, Dumas and Robert Louis Stevenson revealed to me that there also was to be found adventure. No foreigner critical of his fatherland had come to disillusion me. Even my Swiss governess had failed to do that. Indeed, she had actually enhanced the image by her constant assertions of the superiority of Swiss scenery over that of England. Thus my visions of "abroad" continued to retain their exhilarating strangeness, and often some configuration of landscape or architecture, a group of trees, an outline of distant hills, a spire, a tower, caught in some unusual effect of light, would move me to an ecstasy of longing for the day when my visions would materialize.

The fact that this day was now approaching was far from consoling me for my sorrow at the thought of parting from Deniston. Yet, strangely enough, the feelings with which I looked forward to breaking the news of my departure to him were not of wholly unmixed grief. It was going to be, I felt, a dramatic moment. There would be in it an element of romance, the sweet sorrow of parting. There was also a slight sense of superiority involved, for it was I whose schooldays were over, who was going out into the world. It was he who was going to be left behind. There was also, perhaps, a faintly sadistic satisfaction of inflicting sorrow on a friend.

However, when I made the announcement, Deniston's reactions were not quite what I had hoped they were going to be. He neither grew pale, nor did his eyes fill with tears. He merely said, "How absurd!"

"Absurd?" I exclaimed. "What do you mean?"

"I mean it's absurd to be leaving Eton just because your mother thinks it's unhealthy."

This point of view seemed a little to undermine my position.

"Of course, I'm sorry to be leaving Eton," I said, "but I'm going abroad. I'm going to France."

"Well, there's nothing very extraordinary about that," he replied. "Other people have been to France, you know."

I felt constrained to introduce a sentimental note.

"We mayn't perhaps see each other again for years."

"What nonsense!" he retorted. "You talk as if you were going to the other end of the earth. I suppose it's because you've never been abroad before. It only takes an hour to cross the Channel, you know."

I was a little unnerved by his matter-of-fact treatment of the situation and by the intimation that I was making an unnecessary fuss. I abandoned any further attempt to provoke an emotional crisis.

I suppose that I ought to have been pleased at Deniston having taken for granted that my leaving Eton didn't necessarily put an end to our friendship, yet I couldn't help feeling a little hurt at his treating so lightly the possibility that it might. I had hitherto looked upon the absence of sentimentality in his nature as rather an attractive feature. Now that it affected me personally I liked it less. I was led to ponder on a condition of our friendship of which I had always been vaguely conscious. I was fonder of him than he was of me. As I reflected on the matter, it seemed to me that such had been the nature of nearly all my previous friendships. "Dans l'amour il y'a toujours l'un qui baise et l'autre qui tend la joue." The consideration that mine had always been the former role I found a little humiliating. It never struck me that of the two roles the former is the more enterprising, that in friendship, as long as there is no intrusion of jealousy, it is often more blessed to give than to receive.

During the remaining weeks of the term our friendship continued as before, without any variation in its warmth. However, in spite of the assumption that my departure from Eton was not going to affect it, I couldn't help feeling that it was never going to be quite the same. The friendship was so closely bound up with the ambience of Eton, so infused with its atmosphere, that, in other times and in other places, I feared, it could not fail to lose a little of its romantic glamour. I felt the necessity of endeavouring to enjoy to the utmost every moment that remained of it in its present setting, and efforts of this kind, as in the last days of a holiday, are apt to be a little too fevered to be wholly pleasurable.

$( 173 )$

All the while I had been at Eton my affection for it had been growing insensibly. Its beauty, which in the first days had made so forcible an impression on me, I had come to take as a matter of course. It was only at the moment of leaving Eton that I realized to the full my deep attachment to the place, to its buildings, its fields and trees, the river, the surrounding town with the great Castle dominating the horizon, a conglomeration steeped in the romance of bygone centuries. I knew now how much I loved Eton, at all times, at all seasons; the summer sunshine on the playing fields and the river, the bathing at Cuckoo Weir and Athens, the winter fogs and rain that had so often rescued me from football, the walls and cloisters mysterious in lamplight, the darkness of the lanes and passages as one returned in the dusk from outlying class-rooms, and, to descend to more material things, the strawberries-and-cream in the sock-shops and the hot buns at Little Brown's in the mornings before early school.

Eton was for me an Alma Mater beloved for her beauty more than for any other quality, and the memory of it was the most valuable of her gifts.

In so far as my education was concerned, I had learned nothing, less than nothing, a minus quantity. I had lost what little knowledge I had of foreign languages. In history, geography and science I had been confused rather than instructed. I left Eton with a distaste for the Classics and, what was more serious, a distaste for work itself.

No doubt if I had not been prematurely removed from Eton I should be able to speak more favourably of its contribution to my intellectual development. If I had stayed the full course, I might have been induced to take a more earnest view of my studies; I might have made the acquaintance of some of the Eton figures who appear to have had an ennobling influence on one or two of my contemporaries. It was my misfortune that, with the exception of Arthur Benson, I did not enjoy the tuition of anyone I found particularly inspiring.

It would perhaps be difficult to say what sort of education would have been more suitable for a boy of my disposition. My mind and character were of the kind that develop slowly, and it is possible that, had I been more intensively educated at that period of my life, I might have grown up to be, as Herbert Spencer said of early risers, "conceited in the morning and stupid in the afternoon."

That, from a general point of view, my Eton career can hardly be said to have been a very successful one, I have not overmuch regretted. I have known too many men whose lives have suffered from their having been too triumphant in their schooldays. There is a danger in one's golden age coming too early.

Whatever may be its faults, I have never regretted having been to Eton, although I left it as Antony left Cleopatra, with more love than benediction.